Elizabeth von Arnim (1866–19... ...) Beauchamp in Sydney, Australia, ... Travelling in Italy with her father in 1889, she met her first husband, Count Henning August von Arnim-Schlagenthin. They were married in London the following year and lived in Berlin. After five years of marriage the von Arnims moved to their family estate, Nassenheide, in Pomerania: Elizabeth's experience and deep love of Nassenheide were to be wittily encapsulated in her first and most famous novel, *Elizabeth and Her German Garden*, published anonymously in 1898. The twenty-one books she then went on to write were signed 'By the author of Elizabeth and Her German Garden', and later simply 'By Elizabeth'.

Elizabeth von Arnim gave birth to four daughters and a son, whose tutors at Nassenheide included E. M. Forster and Hugh Walpole. Her idyllic Prussian days were, however, to be abruptly ended when, in 1908, debt forced the von Arnims to sell the estate. They moved to England, and in 1910 Count von Arnim died. Buying a site in Switzerland, Elizabeth built the Château Soleil where she worked on her books and entertained such friends as H. G. Wells (with whom she had an affair), Katherine Mansfield (her cousin), John Middleton Murry and Frank Swinnerton. On the outbreak of war she managed to escape to England, but she was unable to rescue her daughter Felicitas, who died in Germany. In 1916 Elizabeth von Arnim married Francis, second Earl Russell, brother of Bertrand Russell, whom she had met three years previously. This proved to be a disastrous union: in the first year of marriage Elizabeth ran away to America, and in 1919 the couple finally separated.

A greatly admired literary figure of her time, described by Alice Meynell as 'one of the three finest wits of her day', Elizabeth spent her later years in Switzerland, London, and the French Riviera where she wrote her autobiography, *All the Dogs of My Life* (1936). On the outbreak of the Second World War she moved to America, where she died two years later at the age of seventy-five.

Virago also publishes ten novels by Elizabeth von Arnim including *Christopher and Columbus* (1994) and *Elizabeth and Her German Garden* (1985).

ALL THE DOGS OF MY LIFE

Elizabeth von Arnim

Published by VIRAGO PRESS Limited March 1995
20 Vauxhall Bridge Road, London SW1V 2SA

Reprinted 1995 (twice)

First published in hardback by William Heinemann 1936

*A CIP catalogue record for this book is available from
the British Library*

Printed and bound in Great Britain by
Cox & Wyman Ltd, Reading, Berkshire

PART I

§

I would like, to begin with, to say that though parents, husbands, children, lovers and friends are all very well, they are not dogs. In my day and turn having been each of the above,—except that instead of husbands I was wives,—I know what I am talking about, and am well acquainted with the ups and downs, the daily ups and downs, the sometimes almost hourly ones in the thin-skinned, which seem inevitably to accompany human loves.

Dogs are free from these fluctuations. Once they love, they love steadily, unchangingly, till their last breath.

That is how I like to be loved.

Therefore I will write of dogs.

§

Up to now I have had fourteen, but they weren't spread over my life equally, and for years and years at a time I had none. This, when first I began considering my dogs, astonished me; I mean, that for years and years

[3]

I had none. What was I about, I wondered, to allow myself to be dogless? How was it that there were such long periods during which I wasn't making some good dog happy?

Lately, in order to answer these questions, I have been casting about a good deal in the past, and in its remoter portions found that the answer to them was my father. There have been other answers of more recent date, as I shall presently explain, but he was the first one. He didn't like dogs. A just but irritable man, with far too few skins really for comfort, noise easily exasperated him, and dogs do often make a noise. Therefore he wouldn't suffer them nearer than out in the back-yard, watching, poor sad beasts, on a chain for the burglar who never came; and if a visitor chanced to bring his dog with him, and it did what perhaps it oughtn't to have done, such as gnaw the rug, or jump up and bark, or, worst of all, omit to remain self-contained, my father, determined that nothing should shake him out of polite-ness, would stand applauding its behaviour so sar-donically, beating his hands gently together, and say-ing at intervals with so awful a mildness, Good dog, Fine little chap, Splendid fellow, that the visit was never repeated.

My mother, too, didn't care about them—or rather, be-ing far too sweet-natured and sunnily pleased with everything to have a feeling so negative as not caring, was simply unaware, I think, of their existence. She didn't seem to know that they too were in the world, breathing the same air, pattering along on their little feet, even as she was, inevitably from birth to death, and I doubt if she had ever stooped and stroked one in her life.

The fact was she was too pretty, too busy with her admirers, to have any time left over for noticing such of her fellow-pilgrims as had more than two legs. A happy, adorable little creature, she went singing through the years, always crowded round by friends and admirers, and never within measurable distance of that secret loneliness, that need for something more than human beings can give, that longing for greater loyalty, deeper devotion, which finds its comfort in dogs. They were nothing to her. Where they were concerned, her imagination, lively enough about other things, became a blank; and since our parents were for us children the supreme authority, the final word, and we reverenced and feared my father, and worshipped my mother, their attitude in all things was our attitude, and what they thought we not merely thought, but passionately upheld.

Therefore dogs were ruled out of the category of possessions we might otherwise have liked to have, and it astonishes me, remembering this, that nevertheless, when

I was quite small, I was given one, and allowed to
keep it.

§

DOG I

Bijou

FOR A BRIEF TIME, for just the time, that is, that it took a
rich young man to court and marry my sister, I was
allowed to keep one because, in the ardour preliminary
to marriage, this young man showered gifts on any of his
beloved's relations who were within reach, and I got a
dog.

There is no way of accounting for its being let in to
the family circle, except that the general atmosphere at
home just then was one of extreme good will and indulgence, the suitor being desirable, and my sister happy.
Also, my father was probably biding his time, knowing
that after the wedding, and the departure of the bride-
groom, all these various gifts could be sorted out and
put in their proper places. Anyhow, I don't think that

my particular gift lasted much beyond the wedding-day, and as I was only five, which isn't at all an age to be trusted with the care and comfort of a dog, it was as well that the first one should have been, presumably, given away. And his stay was so short, and his appearance and disappearance so sudden, that if it weren't for the photograph of us taken together—here it is,—I believe I wouldn't even remember that he had ever existed.

But I do just remember; I do still know that his name was Bijou, and that he was my first. And I also know that I was so frivolous-minded at that period, with so little, if any, sense of real values, that I was actually far more interested, the day we were photographed, in my new yellow boots with tassels to them than in the funny speckled little creature sitting, so good and solemn, at my feet. How very much I have learned since then. How wise I have become on the subject of dogs.

Bijou, then, was my first: a vague small figure, lost now in the mists of time. Between him and my second there was a gulf of nine years, during which I subsisted, as it were, on cats. My father, very luckily, was one of your cat men, so that at least there was always something living about the place which didn't mind, and indeed liked, being stroked and gently tickled. I was the youngest, and alone now at home, handed over to a Mademoiselle whose duty it was to educate me and see that I washed my ears. You can't tickle a Mademoiselle. You can't expect her to turn over and let you stroke her tummy. Besides, I didn't want to stroke it. Therefore these cats came in useful, and I concentrated on them.

But it is a bleak business really, concentrating on cats. One likes response, and there is very little of that to be got out of them. Lofty and aloof, for ever wrapped in remote, mysterious meditation, they allow themselves to be adored, and give hardly anything back. Except purrs. I admit purrs are enchanting, and I used to long to have one myself, but just purrs don't nourish the hungry human heart in search of something to fill its emptiness; and being to all intents and purposes by this time an only child, and my parents absorbed in their particular interests, and my Mademoiselle on the other side of a barrier of French, I did very often feel extraordinarily empty. Besides, how chilling, how snubbing, to be merely looked at when one calls. No blandishments could make those cats stir if they weren't in the mood, and one does want whatever one is calling to *come*. More, one wants it to come enthusiastically, ready for any lark going. One wants, that is, a playfellow, a companion, a friend. One wants, in fact, a dog.

§

DOG II

Bildad

I GOT A DOG. Another one. Number Two. But not till I was fourteen, and had had nine solid years of unadulterated cats.

My father was engaged in going round the world,—an activity which seemed to please him, for he did it twice within my childhood's recollections; and the minute he was gone, relaxation set in. Queer how sprightly life became, how roomy, with what wide margins, when my father, in those years, wasn't there. For my part, instead of taut I became happy-go-lucky; instead of minding my p's and q's and watching my steps, I ceased to mind or watch anything, including the frowns of the Mademoiselle. And when my sister, long since married but still remaining benevolent, offered me a dog, I immediately closed with the offer, not even first asking my mother whether I might accept it.

She, always very sweetly indulgent and easygoing, being so pretty and so much beloved, laughed and kissed me, and said, "Very, well, darling,"—just as though I had begged permission. For she knew my father was still receding and wasn't going to turn his face homewards for at least another six months, and whatever I wanted during that spacious period I took, and my mother laughed and kissed me, and to keep up appearances said, "Very well, darling,"—just as though I had begged permission.

This dog, my second, was Bildad. I have no photograph of him, for he wasn't thought well enough of for anybody to want to take one. He was a small, beige-coloured Pomeranian, about the height of a shoe—prophetically, I now see, Pomeranian, for to Pomerania fate was later going to lead me, and leave me in it for years. It was I who christened him Bildad, being at that time an earnest student of the Bible; and when my Aunts Charl and Jessie, who were spending the day, and had as usual brought their caps with them, in special cap-baskets which opened in the way oysters open when obliged to by fishmongers,—when my Aunts Charl and Jessie asked, "Why Bildad?" I said it was because he was the height of a shoe; and, on their inquiring further, referred them glibly to the Book of Job, second chapter, eleventh verse.

An objectionable child. A pert, unlovable child. My aunts, kindly and indulgent, merely looked at each other, and remarked, for perhaps the hundredth time, that I was a peculiar little thing.

With Bildad, I was blissfully happy. He, unlike Bijou, was a real event in my life. I loved him consciously, and was sure he was the most beautiful of his breed—though knowing what I now know, I see that he wasn't really much of a dog. A Pomeranian never is. Nor is a Pomeranian even a Pomeranian, for when later I became one myself by going to live there, look about me as I might I never saw a dog even remotely resembling Bildad.

But Pomerania, when Bildad became mine, was a

long way ahead of me still. Except for him, I was for several more years entirely out of touch with it. I didn't even know where it was, and I dare say my Mademoiselle didn't either. She, educating me with about as much zeal as I brought to bear on being educated, had a habit, wholly admirable in my eyes, of setting me a page of finger-exercises to practise on the piano, and of French verbs or Latin declensions to be got by heart, and then leaving me alone with Bildad, while she withdrew to her bedroom on her lawful occasions and stayed on there till luncheon.

A mistake to leave me alone with Bildad. Left entirely alone, I might have remained virtuous, but I couldn't with an accomplice. Out through the window—appropriately french—he and I burst the instant we heard the bedroom door shutting, fleeing from pianos, fleeing from verbs and declensions, and rollicked recklessly together on the grass. I knew my Mademoiselle wouldn't come down again till the gong went; I set aside the last twenty minutes for study, arranging to do the finger-exercises at the very end, so that she should find me at the piano, my pigtails vibrating with diligence; and meanwhile we had plenty of time for larks.

How we larked! Rolling over and over, chasing each other in and out of the bushes, throwing stones which we both fetched, and all the time in complete silence—

for Bildad was as well aware as I was that it would be fatal for him to bark. And when we grew tired, or he wished to attend to anything particular of his own, I would stroll among the syringas to cool down, and think, 'Oh, shall I ever have a lover? Oh, shall I?' For in those days, being unacquainted with any, I thought often and highly of lovers.

§

Then my father came back; and the first letter he opened was a bill, inadvertently put among his correspondence, from Marshall and Snelgrove's, for a hundred-poundsworth of just ribbons.

This clouded the home-coming. He hadn't known there were so many ribbons in the world; and for such yards and yards of them to have been used up adorning one small wife left him in a state of frenzied incredulity.

We crept about carefully, trying to pretend we weren't there. By we I mean myself, my Bildad, and my Mademoiselle; though even the adventurous little buyer of ribbons took rather to the tips of her toes. But she had such a way with her when it came to husbands, or indeed to any male, that although we certainly lived for a time in an atmosphere thick with sulphur, she managed, more quickly than most wives would have, to clear it away.

Unfortunately, Bildad was cleared away too. My father, though he couldn't for long withstand my mother's sweet, twining ways, could easily withstand Bildad, and it was no use for that poor dog, whenever he caught a stern eye fixed on him, anxiously to thump his tail on the carpet. Didn't I know, my father inquired of me, his irascible blue eyes flashing, while Bildad withdrew under the nearest table, that dogs weren't allowed in the house? Didn't I know they weren't allowed in the garden either, or anywhere within a mile of him? Would I kindly tell him how it was that when he was not there to keep order, no order was kept?

Trembling I stood, not daring to say a word, for he was the sort of father, frequent in those days, who is never answered back. Besides, what did I know about order, or why it wasn't kept? He only asked me that, I felt, because he didn't care to ask my mother, who, he knew as well as I did, was the real person to inquire of, lest she should temporarily cease to twine; and even then I dimly knew that twining, or not twining, had a lot to do with the family peace.

So presently Bildad was taken off, even as Bijou had been—to a good home, my mother, kissing away my tears, assured me; though of that I wasn't at all certain, because if he had been, and had accordingly been properly exercised every day, wouldn't I have met him sooner or later when I myself was being exercised by my Mademoiselle?

And I never did.

§

But I owed my father no grudge. Such a thing as a grudge against a parent got into few heads at that period. Children were respectful, even in their thoughts. Fathers ordered, and children obeyed. What fathers did was right and unquestioned, and that Bildad should be reft from me had as little of a personal grievance about it as a wet day. And when I grew up, and began to understand him better, and by marrying and going away relieved him of the responsibility that chafed his irritable and conscientious soul, fear of him went, and love took its place. From reverence and fear, I proceeded to reverence and love. Always I had reverenced him; throughout my life he was my ideal of an upright man, of him who does justly, and walks humbly before his God; but now I loved him as well. Deeply. More, at the end, even than I loved my mother if that were possible, taking a great delight, whenever I was able to get away from Pomerania, in his company and conversation. So do we finish up in peace, and in blessing each other from our hearts.

During the last years of all, when everybody who had worried him was either dead or far away, and my mother, long past the ribbon stage, had settled down contentedly to a placid sitting close to him in the sun, they were the most delightful pair of survivors imaginable. True they still didn't like dogs, but I myself by then had grown more mellow, and realised that you can't expect everybody to like everything.

Except for that, they seemed to me quite perfect. No old lady was ever quite so pretty, so gay, so full of fun and laughter as my mother, and no old man was of a riper wisdom than her venerable mate. Gone were their little misunderstandings—I think there must have been many over those admirers of hers, over those persons, that is, for whose further bedazzlement the Marshall and Snelgrove bill was run up,—gone, too, the children who had so frequently exasperated him. He wasn't a man who ought ever to have had any children, except grown-up ones. The cries of babies maddened him. He disliked little girls, who bounced in from the garden without wiping their shoes. Having to provide a Mademoiselle, and then endure her for what no doubt seemed an interminable number of years, gave him no pleasure either. While as for the bills, the endless bills, for boots, for physic, for dentists, for holidays, for mackintoshes and umbrellas, for all the dozens of dull things bright money has to be spent on when there is a family, my father, who was extremely parsimonious while he was well off, and only became freehanded when banks smashed and he grew poor, utterly hated the sight of them.

The days they arrived were black days. Being biblically inclined, my instinct, on such days, was to call upon the hills to cover me; but I refrained, because I knew they wouldn't. Trembling at my own ungodliness, I secretly thought hills were really very like cats, and for all one's calling wouldn't budge. What was the Bible about, I wondered, as respectfully as I could, to suggest that they might? And I made anxious excuses for it, on the ground that perhaps it hadn't known much about geology.

But the years passed, the children took themselves off, or were taken—my case—off, and bills, instead of being for boots, were for bulbs. Nobody who loves his garden as my father did, minds paying for bulbs; on the other hand, few are those who like having to pay for somebody else's boots. Accordingly the clouds, so apt to collect over populous home circles, began to clear away along with the children, and presently there he was, through with all that, sitting peaceful and unruffled among his roses, placidly waiting to die.

He might have been one of the prophets of old, with his snowy beard and domed bald head, except that he was so clean. Never was a man more beautifully, more meticulously clean than my father. He spent a quarter of an hour, every morning, walking up and down his dressing-room brushing his beard, clad in the tomato-coloured silk wrapper he had brought from Japan years before; and on this lavish scale the rest of him was attended to. Inside, too, he was as spotless in his old age as he was outside, washed free, by the mere cessation of annoyances, of everything except benevolence and good-will. When worries left off nagging at him, he had leisure to be what he would have been from the first, if properly let alone—a just man made perfect. I love to remember him as he was those last years, arrived, after much buffeting, in untroubled waters, and with the great blessing of having my happy-minded little mother with him, only wanting to be where he was, and whose very presence in a room seemed to set birds singing.

But to the end they both persisted in having nothing to do with dogs.

§

DOG III

Cornelia

MY THIRD WAS CORNELIA; a black-backed, brown-bellied dachshund, who only understood German. She it was who taught me my first German words, which were *couche*—this doesn't sound very German, but it is,—*schönmachen,* and *pfui.* The last of these three words I ended by finding most useful. Nearly all my domestic problems in Pomerania, I gradually discovered, could be settled by saying very loudly to recalcitrant, neglectful or erring servants, *Pfui.*

Cornelia, though, didn't follow hard on Bildad's heels. There was a gap between his departure and her appearance which I filled by growing up and marrying—or rather being married, because I don't think I had much to do with it; no personal exertion, I mean.

The man who married me was a German, and it was therefore natural that his dog, welcoming me on the threshold of my new home, should be German too. In those days we didn't mind Germans, and my parents saw me being turned into one without flickering an eyelash. I met him while I was being shown Italy by my father, and he, being a person who knew what he wanted, had, it appeared, marked me down as a suitable Pomeranian the very first moment he saw me, though he didn't mention it at once.

He mentioned it very soon, though. Three days later, as he followed me, panting a little, for, like other good Germans in those days who had ceased to be young, he wasn't thin, up the steps of the Duomo in Florence, to the top of which he was taking me in order to show me the view, he was addressing me thus:

"All girls like love. It is very agreeable. You will like it too. You shall marry me, and see." And having arrived at the top, he immediately and voluminously embraced me.

I remember I struggled. Being embraced was entirely new to me, and I didn't at all like it. That he should explain, too, when at last he let me go, that this was but a beginning, alarmed rather than reassured me.

But there was nothing alarming about the ring he pulled out of his pocket and put on my finger, clinching, thus, the business. It was a very lovely sapphire and diamond ring which had belonged to his first wife—he had had one wife already,—and its possession delighted me. I also was delighted by my sudden importance in the family. Up to then I had been nobody, and suddenly to be somebody, or indeed for a time everybody, I must say was very pleasant.

From now on, all that was likely to be of pleasure or profit to me began at once to be done. "The child must be fed," my betrothed, who was immensely older than I was, would say when, passing a pastrycook's in the course of our sight-seeing, I would sniff wistfully.

Quickly I learned to turn my nose this way and that when I smelt anything I wanted to eat, and my father, who had never encouraged eating between meals, found himself obliged to take me into the place the smell was issuing from, and look on with pursed lips while I, no doubt greedily, gulped down cakes.

"The child must go to Bayreuth," my betrothed further announced, having discovered that I loved music; and accordingly when July came, my father, who hated them, found himself attending operas.

"The child must have a dog," was the next announcement after the Bayreuth one, while we were still in Florence, I having shown a violent interest in some passing puppy; and accordingly a dog arrived, a gift from him, and my father had to pretend that he would let me keep it.

But the minute its giver had left us, gone back to

Pomerania to look after the great tracts of rye I was afterwards to know so well—*Animus tuus ego,* was my last bit of advice to him as he left, hastily sweeping together such crumbs of Mademoiselle's Latin as were strewn about my mind into a brilliant whole,—the minute he left, his present was sent back to the place where he had bought it. My father was adamant; I saw for myself that taking a dog about in trains and hotels was difficult; and I parted from it with the greater filial obedience that I had had it too short a time even to get used enough to its name to be able now to remember it.

Thus did I become engaged, and presently was married and removed to Pomerania; and standing on the steps of the remote and beautiful old house—here it is—

in which I was to spend so many happy years, was Cornelia.

§

We immediately loved. At sight we loved. She too had belonged to that previous wife whose traces were everywhere. My opinion of previous wives, high already because of the ring, leapt to heaven when I saw Cornelia. Far, far better than any ring was that blessed little low-geared dog. She whimpered round me, in delighted recognition that here at last was a playmate and friend. Her whole body was one great wag of welcome. She showed off. She did all her tricks. She flung herself on her back, so that I might see for myself how beautiful her stomach was—

"Do not," interrupted my husband, "kiss the dog. No dog should be kissed. I have provided you, for kissing purposes, with myself."

Such was the way he talked. Apophthegms. And I used to listen to them with a kind of respectful amusement, my ear cocked, my head on one side. From the very beginning, I enjoyed and treasured his apophthegms.

§

That first year of marriage, Cornelia and I were everything to each other. Alone all day from directly after breakfast till evening, because my husband went off early to inspect his remoter farms and didn't come back till dark, if I wished to talk I had to talk to Cornelia.

Dogs being great linguists, she quickly picked up English, far more quickly than I picked up German, so we understood each other very well, and *couche, schönmachen,* and *pfui* continued for a long time to be my whole vocabulary.

Fortunately, we liked the same things. She only wanted to be out of doors in the sun, and so did I. Expeditions to the nearer woods soon became our daily business, and the instant my husband, in his high cart, had lurched off round the first corner, we were off round the opposite one, disappearing as quickly as we could, almost scuttling, in our eagerness to be gone beyond reach and sight of the servants.

These servants, I thought I observed, had an apparently insatiable desire to be given orders. As long as I was in the house they followed me about, unintelligibly inquiring. I had a great wish to tell them to *couche.* I felt that if only, at the magic word, they would lie down and stretch themselves out in silence, we should all be a good deal happier. Much, indeed, could they have learned from Cornelia. I believe, for instance, that I would have been wax in their hands if, instead of waylaying me with aggrieved faces, they had simply sat up and begged.

There was a fat little functionary called the *Kalte Mamzell,* who attended exclusively to sausages and sauerkraut—to all those cold things stored in a room of their own for winter use,—who would have been irresistible sitting up and begging, I thought, as I dodged my way to the nearest door, closely followed by Cornelia. Why didn't she? I might, overcome by the spectacle, have given her an order if she had. But anyhow, I would add, so as to get rid of the feeling of guilt, of shirking, of being a fleeing *Hausfrau,* it wasn't really to be expected of me, whose whole life till then had been spent receiving orders, that I should suddenly turn round and give them. These things can't be done in such a hurry. One has to get one's breath. Only six months before, my Mademoiselle had been addressing me as a *petite sotte,* and commanding me to go upstairs at once and wash. How could a person, used to that sort of thing, all at once start looking lofty, and issuing decrees to people manifestly twice her age?

Convinced that this particular person couldn't, I

would make for the open; and once in it, once safe, how happy Cornelia and I were! We frisked across the unreproachful fields, laughing and talking—I swear she laughed and talked,—to the cover of the nearest wood. The world was all before us, and my pockets bulged with biscuits and bones which, when sorted out, would be our several luncheons. What could be more perfect? Nothing, out there, minded what we did. Nothing wanted to be given orders. The March wind, blowing my skirt all anyhow, and causing Cornelia's ears to stream out behind her, didn't care a fig that I was a fleeing *Hausfrau;* the woods, when we got to them—those clear light woods of silver birches, free from obscuring undergrowth,—welcomed us with beauty, just as though I were as deserving as anybody else. Pale beauty it was, in a pale sun; beauty of winter delicately dying, of branches bare, except for mistletoe. But beneath the branches were the first signs of spring, for down among last year's dead leaves, in groups, in patches, in streams, and in some places in lakes, hepaticas were beginning to cover the ground with their heavenly blue.

I would sit in great contentment on a tree-stump, munching my biscuits and staring round at these things, while Cornelia, in great contentment too, but for different reasons, busied herself digging holes and burying her dinner-bones; and I often wondered, I remember,

whether any human being could be happier than I was
then. Happy indeed, at such moments, seemed my lot.
The sun was warm, spring was just round the corner,
I had a kind, indulgent husband who was nearly always
somewhere else, and there wasn't a soul in sight except
a dog.

I asked nothing better of life. I still ask nothing better
of life. Strange to say—for surely it is strange not to
have increased one's claims, during the passage from
youth to maturity?—these very things, just sun on my
face, the feel of spring round the corner, and nobody
anywhere in sight except a dog, are still enough to fill
me with utter happiness. How convenient. And how
cheap.

§

In the afternoons, having come back to the house
much more slowly than we left it, Cornelia and I drove
out. We took the air in an open basketwork carriage
with scarlet wheels, known as the *Viersitzer* and drawn
by a pair of rough-coated, stout horses who looked, I
thought, very like carthorses. It was driven by the
ancient family coachman, and in winter he was dressed
like a penwiper. Multitudinous layers of cloth capes one
over the other, all frilled and sticking out, concealed

him, and from the top of these emerged, as it were the button that finishes off, his antiquated, but still impressive, cockaded top hat.

I soon grew to love him. He was the kindest, gentlest of men, filled with an inexhaustible patience towards her whom he, like my Aunts Charl and Jessie, must also quite often have regarded as a peculiar little thing, and his name was Johann.

> *Johann, Johann,*
> *Du süsser Mann!*

I used to croon to myself, when I got as far as making couplets in German.

"Frau Gräfin wünscht?" he would say, turning round on his box, and beaming down at me.

"What is that bird?" I would ask, to cover my embarrassment.

"That," he would answer, having duly listened to the distant cry—and it didn't matter if it was the cry of a hawk, or an eagle, or a wild goose,—"that," he would answer, delighted to be able to impart information, "is a finch."

But this was much later, when I had collected enough German to ask questions. We went for many drives before I could do that, and the drives were daily, because of the horses having to be exercised. Set aside for my special use, it was my duty to take this particular pair out. I couldn't shirk it, though often I would have liked to, because if I did even for a single afternoon, on the next one they kicked, and the *Viersitzer,* new in the seventies, which was the peak period of the family's glory, could no longer bear much, and therefore it, and Cornelia, and Johann and I were in peril, on such occasions, of being destroyed.

This was a lesson I quickly learnt. Diligently every day I drove out, whether I wanted to or not; and there were tarnished silver coronets all over the harness, and Johann's hat and whip were decorated with frayed cockades in the family colours, and in this condition of shabby splendour—there was everything in profusion on the estate except money,—we proceeded to do that which was necessary to calm the horses, by exploring the nearer portions of the forest that lay along our northern boundary.

This forest was immense. It stretched away uninterruptedly to the north, till stopped by having got to the shores of the Baltic. We had it all to ourselves. Unnoticed, except by what Johann called finches, we passed along its vistas, and no human eye beheld the capes, the coronets and the cockades. In that past which seemed to me at my age remote, these things had all been new and spick and span, because of the glory which for a time was the portion of the family; and when, having risen and blazed, the glory at last faded out, it left a litter behind it, in every stage of decomposition, for the ulti-mate use, so it appeared, of one small foreign girl and one small indigenous dachshund. Even Johann's capes hadn't been renewed since the seventies; and sitting behind him, and the air passing through their voluminous folds before reaching me, I could smell the careful camphor they had been preserved in during innumerable summers. Gone were the days when new capes were provided each winter as a matter of course. The evil times had come of eking out, of making do. At least, my husband seemed to regard the times we had arrived at as evil, but that was because he was in the unfortunate position of having a past to compare them with. I, who had practically no past, and whose family had never fallen from glory for the reason that it had had no glory to fall from, thought the times wholly delightful; and anyhow I rather liked camphor.

§

When we had got sufficiently far into the forest to have lost sight of the last of our farms, we used to get out and walk, Cornelia and I, she padding along beside me, her funny little turned-out toes making no sound in the deep sand, while the carriage followed at a respectful distance—for everything was respectful in Pomerania, even the distances, and I was abashed by the amount of respectfulness lavished on me, who had so lately been a *petite sotte,* from morning till night.

We always walked northwards, and however far we walked we never got to where the trees left off and the sea began. Nor did we ever meet a soul, because, as I presently learned, there weren't any to meet. Not in the forest. Not nearer than eleven miles to the northeast, where the head forester lived.

How beautiful this security seemed to me, this enchanting security of knowing oneself unnoticed and unseen! And not only was the forest empty of human beings, but our nearest neighbour on the other side, the side of open plains and rolling rye-fields, was ten miles away along almost impassable rutted tracks—the one neighbour, that is, of our own class, which was *hochgeboren.* Other neighbours there were, much nearer, some only two miles off and easily accessible because they lived on the high road, but they were no good to us because they were only *wohlgeboren.* For purposes of social intercourse, *Wohlgeborens* were of no use at all. If the *Hochgeborens* happened to meet them in a train or other public place, they were, of course, gracious, almost crushingly gracious, but they never invited them to dinner; and having myself become *hochgeboren,* through what seemed to be no fault of my own, I found that it was one of my duties, and an immediate and pressing one, to learn and practise this graciousness trick, while being at the same time careful not to commit myself to anything really warming, like food.

It was very difficult. It took me years,—far longer than picking up German. And once I had learned it, I found it equally difficult to unlearn. Heavens, how it stuck! For instance when, in the fulness of time, I became widowed and went back to England to live, for quite a long while I would surprise my friends by the extreme courtesy with which, though they were usually already doing it, I indicated that they might sit down.

It was when I at last began to realise how deeply involved I really was in a web of rules of correct behaviour, that I first became aware of the magnificent freedom of dogs. I had loved Bildad, and I did love Cornelia—Bijou was too far down the years to count,— with all my heart, but now I envied them as well. Nobody expected anything of dogs. Whatever they did which might perhaps, according to our ideas, be not quite nice, was put down to their being, precisely, dogs, and thought no more of. See them in the morning, I

used to say to myself, my envious eye on Cornelia,—
see them jump out of their baskets, and with a single
shake be at once ready for a new day, while I had to be
put through the most irksome washings, and combings,
and tyings-together, before the German maid, whose
presence prevented any skimping, considered me fit to be
seen. See them, too, at meal-times, swallowing their
food and done with it, while I, sitting solemnly at a
table, had to wait, however hungry or greedy I might
be, till servants in white gloves—much darned,—and
many coroneted buttons—own brothers to the tarnished
ones on Johann,—presented me, at proper intervals,
with dishes. And see them, most enviable of all, having
met with disapproval, set everything right by simply
getting up on their little haunches and begging, or by
apologetically wagging their tail.

If only, *only* I too had a tail, I used to sigh, when I had
offended, always mysteriously, always without the least
notion why or how, the Frau Director, or the Frau Inspector, or the Frau Vieharzt, or any of the numerous
Fraus who seemed to infest the place—how vigorously
I would wag it! So anxious was I after a while, when at
last I had learned that behave according to the rules I
simply must, or bring disgrace on the whole class of
Hochgeborens besides probably being hounded out of

Pomerania, that I would gladly have sat up and begged for hours if it would have placated anybody.

In the end, though, once I had got the lesson well by heart, the mellifluousness of my manners had to be seen to be believed; and directly I could talk German I was able to wind my way in and out of the most lengthy and intricate politenesses, and bring out my verb all proper in its place, at the finish, with the best of them.

§

Just about the time I had my first baby, Cornelia had hers; but there were six of them, to my one. It might have been supposed, seeing she had six, that she would have taken six times as long to get over her confinement as I did, who had only produced one. Not at all. She was up and about and as lively as ever within a week, while I wouldn't like to count the weeks it took me to be merely up and about, let alone as lively as ever. I don't think I was ever quite as lively as ever again. Lively, yes; but not as ever. Cornelia had lost her fellow-larker for good and all. If she wanted to lark, which she did almost at once, she had to lark alone. I stayed at home. I hung over cradles, doting. As far as Cornelia was concerned I had gone for good, disappeared behind a steadily increasing cloud of babies. Even her puppies didn't interest me, so much absorbed was I in that equivalent of puppies which kept on, year in year out, appearing from God knew where. Indeed, my time was so much taken up by these crowding arrivals, this brood of astonishing little strangers collecting round me, that I presently forgot her altogether. She faded from my consciousness. The part of me which had adored her went to sleep. And when it woke up, the children being older and I with more leisure to look round, and I asked, suddenly perturbed, "But what has become of Cornelia?" she was dead.

Then I was sorry; sorry, and ashamed. Uncomfortable to realise how selfish, how indifferent to those who were once one's friends, absorption in family life can make one. Cornelia deserved better of me than that I should exclude, neglect, and forget her. For a whole year she had been my close companion, devoted to me, looking to me for all her fun and happiness, and providing me with very nearly all mine. Was it well done, directly I had something else to love, to drop her out of my life? I might at least have taken her for a run sometimes, or had her in to tea, and stroked her silken ears; but—"Dogs," my husband had laid down after my first child was born, emitting another apophthegm when Cornelia, leaving her own flock, came up to visit me, "are fatal to infants." And since being too ignorant to check his statements I found it easier to believe than inquire into them, I let her be shoo'd away, and that was the beginning of her end.

§

DOG IV

Ingraban

IT MAY BE LAID DOWN as a sound principle that nobody should keep a dog who isn't prepared, not only to take personal care of it, but to love it. You can't take personal care of it, nor can you really love it as it deserves to be loved, if you are taking care of and loving a crowd of tiny children. There simply isn't time.

It wasn't, then, because of my husband's theory that dogs were fatal to the young that I did without any for the next few years, for on thinking it over, and observing the abundance of healthy children in the villages, and also the simultaneous abundance of dogs, I left off

believing it; but it was simply for want of time that between Cornelia and Ingraban there was a space of ten
years. Then, when the last of my first batch of children
had disappeared into the schoolroom, and my next batch
hadn't begun to appear yet, my thoughts once more
wandered to dogs.

I needed a companion. My husband still went off
directly after breakfast to his distant farms, and the
mornings, when I had done weighing-out sausages and
counting sheets—for by now my responsibilities had
been faced and accepted,—were long. I needed something that had to be exercised, and therefore gave me an
excuse for getting off to the woods myself; and since I
was young—it took me a terrible time to leave off being
young,—the companion couldn't be a pleasant youth,
as I might perhaps have liked, because that would have
set the Frau Director and the Frau Inspector and the
Frau Vieharzt too much agog, but must be something
beyond the reach of calumny.

Nothing is so entirely beyond the reach of calumny
as dogs; in fact, they seem to have all the privileges and
exemptions that are most worth having. Ingraban and I
could spend whole days together, and at night he could
sleep on the rug by my bed, without a word being said.
He was a Great Dane; a huge, lovely beast, of the colour
called *isabelle*. I got him from a breeder in the nearest

big town, and he was one of a series, born of the same parents, whose names all began with *I*. I paid two hundred marks for him, and brought him home, clutching his collar, half triumphant and half scared, in the *Viersitzer*.

"Die kleine Frau und der grosse Hund," was my husband's apophthegm when, benevolent but abstracted, for he was thinking of his rye, he first saw us together.

With Ingraban magnificently slouching beside me, I could go anywhere, however far away and lonely. He was my protector, as well as my friend. Tramps, from the day he came into my life, held no more terrors for me. Those fears which, I suppose, most women know who walk alone in solitary places, left me. I didn't any longer jump if I heard what sounded like a footstep; I didn't any longer pause and listen with a beating heart, if something moved in the bushes. Ingraban would deal with all that. Ingraban, you could see by just looking at him, was prepared to deal with anything. Yet how gentle he was to me and to the children, how considerate and how kind. He was also more intelligent by a good deal, I later discovered, than Great Danes usually are, so that really I was very lucky. The perfect dog, I thought. And as he sat on his haunches beside me in the *Viersitzer* of an afternoon, during those drives which still continued, because still the horses had to be exercised, as he sat proud and splendid, watchful yet motionless, towering above my head, reaching well up to Johann's capes, I reflected how infinitely superior he was to those three small creatures of my past, Bijou, Bildad, and Cornelia. 'Give me big dogs every time,' I said to myself, ungrateful, as one so often is, to the past when pleased with the present, and not yet knowing how stupid big dogs can be.

But there was one flaw in Ingraban's perfections: he couldn't see deer unmoved. The fields were full of fallow-deer—small, elegant creatures with faces very much the colour of the ripening rye they peeped out at us from, and he, brought up in the suburbs of a big town, had never met any till he came to me, and found them irresistible.

It was to be his undoing. Perhaps if they had stayed quiet where they were he might have been saved, but when they saw the *Viersitzer* appearing they invariably leapt away, and instantly Ingraban, regardless of my impassioned orders, hurled himself after them.

Perfectly obedient in every other way, on this one point he was incorrigible. I did all I could to cure him, not because I had any idea it would be his undoing, but because, as the good wife of an agricultural husband, it seemed awful to me that rye should be trodden down. *Animus tuus ego*—the injunction was of the first importance to us, who drew most of our sustenance from rye; and I would adjure and scold, and I would seize his collar, only to find it wrenched free with hardly any effort, and chastise him when at last he came back, hurting my hand horribly, and him not at all. And one day, when he was off at such a rate and so far that in a flash he was no longer anywhere to be seen, I heard a distant shot, and it wasn't a deer which had been killed, but Ingraban. He lay dead, when we reached him, a bleeding hole in his beautiful, smooth side.

"How could you—oh, how *could* you!" I cried, beside myself, to the shooter, who was standing looking on and lighting a cigarette.

"Er jagte," was all he said, indifferently.

And why should he not be indifferent? Before him was only a decrepit old coachman, and an obviously foreign young woman. Old men and women. He wasn't going to waste words, or offers of help, on such as those. If Johann and I had been somebody in uniform instead of what we so evidently were, persons unable to do anything but protest—and Johann didn't even do that, being disciplined in acceptance,—he would probably have made some apology, and perhaps lent a hand in the ghastly, the almost impossible task, of lifting the poor, bleeding body into the *Viersitzer*.

Things being as they were, he walked away.

[*40*]

§

DOG V

Ingulf

I HAVE no picture of Ingraban, but here is one of his successor, Ingulf—a sad dog, a dog who during the whole of his short stay with me never cheered up once.

See how solemn he looks in the snapshot, turning his back on me, taking no interest in whatever I was doing with my little son.

I thought it was because he was so big. He was the biggest dog I have ever had, and his great body seemed from the first to depress him, and be a trouble to drag about. Far from wanting to chase deer, he stared at them springing across the fields with a lack-lustre eye. A sad, apathetic dog, sitting down whenever he could, and getting up reluctantly.

Ingraban's death had shocked me very much, and my husband, seeing this, began comforting me, and one thing led to another in the way things do, and before I knew where I was I was caught once more in the toils of childbearing. A strange form, I thought, as I dealt as best I could with the aches and pains, the dark forebodings and tendency to make Wills, which always, in my case, went with that condition—a strange form for comfort to take. Still, there it was, and it certainly did for a time make me forget Ingraban. But when it was over, and I had begun to crawl out into freedom again, and presently to walk out, and again presently, with something of my old confidence in life, to run out, how much I missed him, how big and lonely the woods felt without his company and protection!

It wasn't, though, till my second batch of children—

if that can be called a batch which consists of two,—was well on its stout little legs and rushing about the nursery breaking things, that I allowed myself to consider a successor to him. Up to then I had, like a solicitous hen, hovered; but when the cradles became cots, and the cots beds, and their contents spilled themselves riotously all over the place, I thought I might have a day off now and then; and for days off, there is nothing like dogs.

True there were three sturdy elder children, dying to have days off with me, but they, poor unfortunates, weren't available, because by that time they were being held down by tutors and governesses. In the schoolroom they sat throughout the mornings, racked by watchful pedagogic eyes, whatever might be going on outside in the way of sunshine and fresh, sweet winds. During the afternoons, ponies were brought and they were taught to ride, rackets were provided and they were taught to play tennis. At stated times they were taken to the nearest pond, and taught to swim. At other stated times they were brought back, shown grasses and flowers, and taught to botanize. Two tutors, one German and one English, and two governesses, one German and one French, presided over these carefully arranged activities. The children were being educated according to a plan my husband had drawn up, when first we were married, for the education of those sons who had all turned out to be daughters, and he wasn't going to have it wasted. Therefore he made the best of the lamentable situation by persuading himself that, given the same training, whether a girl was a boy or not, the results would be the same.

I don't know whether this is so. It wasn't so, anyhow, in our case. In spite of the classes gone through at home being exactly the same as those the boys in the State schools were going through, in spite of the yearly examinations in the county town, whither, just before Christmas, the children were led in order to pass them, there were no results. Not, that is, the sorts of results my husband and the German tutor would have called good. It seemed as if, firmly rooted in our three little daughters, was that which resisted the acquisition of facts, and was entirely indifferent to the shame of not passing examinations.

At first this upset me, and I deplored that these dear beings, the source of so much joy and pride to me, should, offered the means of grace, flatly refuse to have anything to do with them. But presently I was thankful, for it was a serious business in Germany being educated like a boy, especially if you weren't one, and dreadful stories were going about of little boys who, having strained every nerve to acquire and absorb, and yet failing, killed themselves. One, the son of a distant relative, was found hanging on an apple-tree in his father's orchard. Another ended miserably in the Oder. Naturally, then, on hearing these things, I left off deploring, and rejoiced instead when, regularly every year, my children were either turned down or came out bottom.

Their father, though, minded very much, and so did their German tutor, whose job it was to keep them up to the mark they ought, according to their age, have reached. Their father, indeed was violently annoyed, said they were *dumme Weiberswesen,* regarded the current German tutor as responsible for their being so, and dismissed him.

What, inquired the English tutor—that youth, alternately from Oxford and Cambridge, who came for six months at a time to read the prose and poetry of their mother's tongue with the children,—was all the fuss about?

What, inquired the French governess, would be the good of having passed all these examinations *lorsque ces pauvres petites feront leurs premières couches?*

And the German governess, who was amorously disposed, and fell in love with each German tutor in turn, passionately took the dismissed one's part, following him about like a dog, and, as it were with loud barks, proclaimed it was entirely the children's fault, who were incorrigible idlers.

Perhaps they were; but how much better to be an idler than end on an apple-tree, or in the Oder. And it was the way poor Fräulein Pöckel was behaving, for ever at the heels of him who was about to leave, which made me remember dogs again, and think how nice it would be to be followed about myself by something devoted, but by something, in my case, with four feet. Those boxed-up children of mine, never to be got at; the little second batch in the nursery, for years still unavailable;—if I wanted a companion, plainly it must be one of the happy, care-free race which can't be made to do lessons. It must, that is, be a dog.

"One wants to be *complete*," I burst out suddenly one day at the evening meal, at which sat, as usual, the three elder children, their parents, their tutors, and their governesses.

I can't think why I didn't simply say one wants a dog. The way I put it sounded like almost anything—like *femmes incomprises,* like women thwarted and untenderly used.

It was a great success, though, that remark, with the the governesses, who groaned agreement.

"*Ach ja!*" sighed the German one, fixing her gaze on the new German tutor, who fixed his on his plate, for he was a candidate for Holy Orders, and accordingly cautious.

"*Dieu, que c'est vrai,*" muttered the French one, casting up her eyes.

The English tutor looked at me a little curiously. Having been with us nearly three months, he knew that nothing was ever said or discussed, much less burst out, at those meals, which had to do with anybody's private feelings. At them, twice a day, the parents were accustomed to address courteous commonplaces in turn to each of the *Lehrkraft,* as the tutors and governesses collectively were called, and sometimes even to make small jokes, which were received with the same kind of eager appreciation to be observed in Law Courts, when the Judge condescends to pleasantry. The father, that is, made small jokes; the mother was too much oppressed by the ceremoniousness of the meal to be merry. What happened at breakfast and tea when the parents were alone, the English tutor didn't, of course, know, but anyhow, whenever he was present, they were both impeccably *hochgeboren.*

Now here was one of them, having a lapse. No wonder he looked up curiously, and with new interest. Also, the agreeing groans of the governesses rather suggested that reserve might be about to be thrown off, and the decorous dinner-table flooded in another instant by released feminine suppressions. So that, being young and graceless, he was pleased.

[47]

But he was reckoning without the Graf. That deft handler of situations into which his wife got him said, while the obedient laughter rippled round the table again, *"Meine liebe kleine Frau,* help yourself to another of these admirable pancakes, and then you will be complete."

Afterwards in the library, when half-past eight had struck, and the governesses, on hearing it, had arisen, collected their charges, bowed good-night, and departed through one door, while the tutors were simultaneously bowing good-night and departing through the other, he said, hopefully, "What is this about wanting to be complete? Is it, my Small, that you perhaps wish for another child?"

And he was, I am afraid, very much disappointed, in spite of there already being five children, when I explained that all I wanted was a dog.

§

Next day I got into the *Viersitzer,* and once more visited the breeders from whom I had bought Ingraban. There I immediately fell in love with Ingulf. Here he is, with my youngest little daughter vainly trying to have

a bit of fun with him; and here he is again [next page], with the same little daughter, still not looking at all pleased:

I think it was his size that swept me off my feet. Liable to be overlooked myself, how can I help admiring the impressively evident? Ingulf was evident indeed. Of the same ancestry as Ingraban, coming under the same letter of the alphabet, he was half as big again as his predecessor and looked like a small pony, and no doubt it was his being half as big again as Ingraban which made his price be half as much again. Probably, I thought, the price was measured by his inches; or was it measured by my patent eagerness? Anyhow, I bought him.

By that time I was earning money writing stories, and didn't feel so awful about spending a little as I used to at the beginning of my life in Pomerania, and the *Viersitzer,* almost entirely filled with dog, heaved off triumphantly homewards.

Doubts very soon, though, began to lay hold of me; even then, as early as that homeward journey, they began to. For wasn't it a little strange that this dog, entirely unaccustomed to being taken for a drive, shouldn't mind the *Viersitzer,* shouldn't, indeed, appear to mind anything? He was neither afraid nor pleased; he was simply indifferent. There he sat drooping beside me, an immense mass of dejected dog, and no need at all for me to hang on to his collar as I had had, with all my strength, to hang on to Ingraban's on our first journey together. Useless to pat, to flatter, to try to encourage with bright talk of bones and dinner. Nothing had the least effect on him. He didn't move; he took no interest; I don't believe he so much as listened. With a lack-lustre eye that great dog stared in front of him, showing no sign of life even when a hare darted straight across our path; and the first thing he did, when we reached home, was to lie down.

Quite unnecessary to order Ingulf to *couche;* he was always already doing it. Quite unnecessary, either, ever to say *pfui* to him, for he was a most virtuous dog, protected from sin by absence of desires. What a contrast to his impassioned predecessor! Could it be that my lovely new dog wasn't intelligent? Or did he merely need feeding up?

Since I couldn't bear the thought of his not being intelligent, I began diligently feeding him up. I also diligently exercised him. He ate what was set before him apathetically, and apathetically he followed when I took

[51]

him out. But it was difficult to exercise him properly, because he was so big that even if I ran—and I was for ever running, in my zeal for his welfare,—he still, to keep up with me, needed only to walk, and if I paused for any reason, such as getting my breath or having to tie my shoelace, instantly he lay down.

The vet was fetched.

"Freely this dog must be fed," he pronounced, after examining him.

"But he is," I said.

"Movement, then, is what he requires."

"But he is always being moved."

"Then it is worms he suffers from, and I will send medicine."

The medicine came, was given, and not a worm resulted. Food in increasing quantities was brought, and languidly, but obediently, eaten. Like a dog in a dream he did whatever was required of him, eating, slouching out for walks, eating again, and on every possible occasion immediately lying down.

"*I* don't know what to do with him," I at last confessed.

"Poor little one," said my husband, trying to comfort me; but by this time I was wary of comfort, and evaded it.

"Perhaps," I said a few days later, disconsolately gazing at Ingulf, who was lying down, "I had better take him back."

"Certainly," agreed my husband, who was all for taking dogs back.

"And exchange him."

"No, not exchange him."

It was a long while, though, before I could bring myself to part from Ingulf. I couldn't help thinking there must be a lot in him, if only I knew how to get at it. So much dog, so manifestly roomy, and with such a splendid head, was unlikely to be just empty. It was my fault, for not knowing how to stir him up.

But something told me that, try as I might, I would never be able to stir up Ingulf. He was permanently, congenitally, a sad, indifferent dog. And one afternoon, both of us equally silent and depressed, we travelled back together to the place he had come from.

The breeder, who had advanced smiling, ceased to smile when he saw what was with me.

"I think perhaps he is a little old," I began, on whom this truth had gradually been dawning.

"Old?"

"Old," I said, trying to face an eye, become indignant, without flinching. All my life I have found it difficult to face indignant eyes. Fortunately there haven't been many, up to now, to face.

"You say old?" he asked, as one asks who cannot rightly believe his ears.

"I did say old," I confessed, fighting against an inclination to look somewhere else.

Then he opened Ingulf's jaw, and requested me to examine his teeth; which I did, and was none the wiser.

Then he requested me to feel certain muscles; which I did, and still was none the wiser.

"This dog," he asserted loudly, straightening himself —and none can be more loud than your German, nor more menacingly straighten himself,—"was quite recently a newborn."

I couldn't meet his eye, it was so indignant. Only by fixing my own on Ingulf, who was lying down, had I the courage to murmur something to the effect that years slip by in the oddest way when one is busy, and before one has noticed what they are doing they have accumulated and disappeared.

At that he straightened himself even more, and with his hands on his hips stared at me in so dreadful a silence that I, anxious to avoid whatever might be coming next, explained quickly the real purpose of my visit. It was, I said, to buy—I had no heart any more for the word exchange,—another dog.

In the end I bought two. Puppies. Most adorable, but

two. Enough to melt a heart of stone, but still two. What, at home, was going to be the reaction? With what apophthegm would they be greeted? Well, never mind that now, I thought, fumbling for the money.

They cost half as much again as Ingulf, because of there being two. Evidently, the breeder pointed out, seeing that I had arrived with only one dog and was going away with two, I ought, in justice, to pay twice as much, but, as I appeared to be turning into an old customer, he would make a concession.

At that I began murmuring again,—something, this time, about going away with only one dog really, because of leaving Ingulf behind. But he would have none of this, and I felt myself that it needed thinking out. Besides, it wasn't a good moment for reasoning and argument, for the puppies, who were about the size of sheep, were being hoisted into the *Viersitzer,* only immediately to fling themselves out of it again on the other side.

Our drive home was punctuated by escapes and recaptures. Several times the horses tried to bolt. From opposite sides of the *Viersitzer* puppies, who seemed suddenly to have become dozens, with hundreds of legs and thousands of excited tails, leapt and larked off into the undergrowth. I was kept much too busy jumping out after them, and breathlessly bringing them back, to bother any more about the sort of reception they and I would get when we arrived.

It was less cordial, even, than I had feared. My husband, back from his daily tour of inspection, unfortunately came out to greet me, and before the horses had pulled up out tumbled the puppies, wrenching themselves free of the collars I was hanging on to, and hurling themselves joyously straight at him.

Naturally he was upset.

§

DOGS VI AND VII

Ingo and Ivo

THESE PUPPIES were called Ingo and Ivo. They belonged to the same *I* class as Ingulf and Ingraban, and were just on six months old when they plunged, so violently, into my life.

[56]

I have various pictures of them during their time
with me, which lasted three years. Here is one—taken
during a moment, rare indeed at the beginning, of re-
pose. The woman, I regret to say, is myself. I think I
was uglier then than I have, perhaps, sometimes been
since; but I daresay I wasn't.

Here is another—with my two youngest children in
the background. For the youth holding the stick I
wasn't responsible,—I mean, he wasn't mine; though
when I look at the last photograph, I admit that anything might have been possible to me in the way of
progeny. However, he was only the pantry boy.

Here is one of Ingo, later on, with my little son:

And here is one of Ivo, also later on, with the pastor's child, who was spending her birthday with us, and accordingly was wreathed.

Beautiful dogs they grew into, both of them, as any one can see, and a great source of pride to me when at last they had learned to behave.

It took them a long while. I went through much before they did, for by the time I bought them it had become my habit, during such moments as remained after I had housekept, and been a good wife, and been a good mother, and done my duty by the Frau Director and the Frau Inspector and the Frau Vieharzt, to shut myself up and write stories.

In a disused greenhouse out in the garden I shut myself up, and of course the puppies, who were always with me, had to be shut up in it too. This didn't make for peace. Before they came, the greenhouse—here it is—

—had been a calm place; mouldy but quiet, as a commodious grave might be; smelling of the past—again as a grave might,—when long dead gardeners used to place pots in it, long since broken, each with a little plant destined later for the pleasure of long since departed *hochgeborene* mistresses.

In those tranquil, pre-puppy days no sound could be heard there except my pen scratching, for Ingulf, stretched out on a rug, was the last dog to make a sound, and, thankful not to have to walk anywhere or eat anything, lay motionless as a stone. Complete peace, accordingly, prevailed. Undisturbed I wrote. Nobody could look in at me from outside, because the windows were bleared over by the dust of ages, and no servant, driven by an uncontrollable itch to be given some more orders, if he or she came after me could be sure I was there, because Ingulf, convenient dog, averse from the smallest exertion, was to be relied on not to growl, whatever knockings there might be at the locked door. So that all I had to do, when would-be interrupters arrived, was to sit without moving, and pretend I was somewhere else.

Admirable conditions for work. They were put an end to by Ingo and Ivo. Wherever I went for the first week or two after their arrival, whatever cover I took, everybody knew exactly where I was. I was encompassed by a cloud of witnesses, all legs and tails, and neither they nor I could be hid. The corner where the greenhouse was, instead of being the quietest in the garden, became the noisiest. Out of it proceeded almost continual cries of *couche* and *pfui*. Inside it an uproar of enraptured barks, while havoc was being made of the simple furnishings, prevented any possibility of work.

We all calmed down, though, after a bit, though the puppies' first introduction to the greenhouse was a disaster. Some ancient flower-pots, piled forgotten in a corner, and never so much as glanced at by the indifferent Ingulf, were pounced on at once, and routed out and sent flying in pieces by huge puppies drunk with the delight of destruction. The rug on which Ingulf—surely, after all, an admirable dog?—had lain with such quiet dignity, was seized at each end, and tugged exultingly asunder. Short work was made of a cushion which was so unfortunate as to slip off my chair; and finally, leaping up in a paroxysm of high spirits to lick my distracted face, Ivo knocked the table over, and there was a most frightful mix-up on the floor of *Fräulein Schmidt and Mr. Anstruther*—a story I was just then trying to write,—and ink, and broken glass. Could Shakespeare, could Kipling, have worked under such circumstances?

I remember kneeling down to rescue what still remained of Fräulein Schmidt, and seeing, staring up at me where a great splash of ink left off, the remarks she had been making, and I had been writing, when Ivo tumbled her over on to the floor.

A sinner, she said, and I wrote, *should always sin gaily.*

Again: *It's a poor creature,* she said, and I wrote, *who while he sins is sorry.*

Presumably I had agreed with her. Was she not my mouthpiece? The trumpet through which, morning after morning, I so busily blew? Yet here were the gayest sinners, leaping round their committed sins in an ecstasy of not being sorry, and far from admiring them I was so angry that I could hardly get my *pfuis* out fast enough.

Perhaps Fräulein Schmidt wasn't as right always as she thought she was. A little hasty, perhaps, when it came to laying down the law.

Anyhow, for a while I lost faith in her, and broke off communications.

§

It may be laid down as another sound principle, amplifying the one on page thirty-six, that nobody who wishes to work should keep big puppies. Probably no puppies should be kept at all by such a person, but certainly not big ones, and still more certainly not big ones if he, or she, who keeps them is himself, or herself, small.

I was small and still am, and Ingo's and Ivo's faces, when they stood on their hind legs and put their paws on my shoulders—an upsetting way of behaving which I tried to discourage,—were on a level with mine, and however quickly I jerked my head aside it wasn't always quick enough to avoid a lick. Also their tails, which perpetually wagged, wagged across the tops of tables, and swept everything before them.

These two habits alone prevented their being allowed indoors. But there were those other habits, common to all the young, which only growing up would correct. My corrections were no good because, directly I approached to take hold of their collars, and it was evident what I had in mind, they would violently back away; while as for rubbing their noses in anything, no efforts of mine ever succeeded in getting their heads so much as to bend.

Therefore they spent such time as I was housekeeping, eating or sleeping, alone in the greenhouse, and I had to manage as best I could when, after these intervals, I went back to them, not to be knocked over by their joyful welcome. Gradually, however, things settled down. The secret of peace with puppies, I discovered —up to then I had had only ready-made dogs (except Bijou, who doesn't count), and had everything to learn, —is to give them a great deal of exercise, and a great deal of food. They should be gorged; regularly. Then they will sleep for hours—quite long enough, I found, in Ingo and Ivo's case, for me to deal justly with Mr. Anstruther, against whom I had been feeling rather a grudge.

This, then, was the line I took; and presently a new rug was able safely to be put in the greenhouse, and while they lay on it, stupefied by well-being, lost to the world, a relaxed heap of paws and ears and tails, with two tightly-filled bellies to point the moral, I got on, once again, with Fräulein Schmidt.

§

DOG VIII

Prince

MY NEXT DOG was English; and he was English because, three years after Ingo and Ivo arrived, circumstances caused me to cease to be a Pomeranian. We all ceased to be Pomeranians; and, having ceased, the children and I came over to live in England.

Ivo was given to the pastor, and Ingo to the Oberinspektor. They couldn't come with me because of quarantine, but I know their homes were good, and their new owners proud. Indeed, nobody could help being proud of them, such handsome dogs had they grown into. Not very intelligent, perhaps, though definitely more so than Ingulf, but fine, vigorous, upstanding dogs,—the sorts of dogs who, if they had been wives, might have bored a sensitive husband, and thoroughly satisfied a dull one.

Prince was very different. He was a wicked dog, with a hot red eye which made me falter during our preliminary how do you do's. But anyhow my heart was heavy, and not really in the how do you do's, as no doubt he at once knew. I was for ever thinking of that past which only the other day had been the happy present. I kept on looking back at it over my shoulder. It seemed incredible, the suddenness with which an entire ordered, regular existence could be swept away, and all its etiquettes and rigidities. I missed everything. I was sad and lonely. My props had been knocked from beneath me, and instead of props I had responsibilities. Are not five children, the youngest only six, serious responsibilities?

But this isn't autobiography, so I needn't enlarge. All I need say is that life in Devonshire, after life in Pomerania, seemed to go about, as it were, in slippers, and I, so long trained to expect discipline in others, was much shocked when the English gardener, on my first addressing him, instead of springing to attention and clicking his heels together, leaned comfortably on his spade.

Behold us, then, a little flock of Pomeranians, accustomed, in personal intercourse, to rigidities, and at the hands of nature to strong winds, much loose sand flying about, and harsh treatment generally,—behold us arriving, all dressed in black and met by a black dog suspiciously sniffing, in the sticky softness and easy-going ways of Devonshire. There we at once, in spite of not being at all happy, began to grow fat, seduced by junkets and their rich, accompanying cream; there, after years of practically complete freedom from invitations owing to lack of *hochgeboren* neighbours, I found myself entangled in tea-parties; and it was there that I first astonished callers by my Junker habit, contracted during long years of association with the Frau Director and the Frau Inspector and the Frau Vieharzt, of graciously conveying to them that they might sit down.

At all this Prince looked on with a hot, red eye. His business was to be my companion when the children, their German *Lehrkraft* shed for ever, were at a daily school, and accordingly he was present, wary and distrustful, when I went round returning calls. Unfortunately, he and I liked each other less and less. Black as the devil, closely curled over by what looked like astrachan, his head and face were smooth, and this made them seem out of proportion small compared with the rest of him. From his head his body sloped upwards to his tail, which gave him a lowering, furtive look. He was five years old; much too old for me to do anything with him really, even if I hadn't, each time I caught his red eye, been inclined to recoil. Dogs always know if one is inclined to recoil. It isn't necessary to do it visibly, because, should there be the least recoil anywhere inside one, they know about it at once. With dogs it has to be through and through genuine affection and confidence or nothing, and it quickly became clear to me that, as far as Prince was concerned, it was going to be nothing.

Nevertheless, accustomed to a dog at my heels, I took him with me when first I began returning the innumerable calls, leaving him in the pony-carriage—I now went about in a pony-carriage which was rather like a dachshund, it was so low on the ground, and in my German weeds I think I must have looked as if I were an early edition of Queen Victoria,—while I was in the different houses; and the retired colonels, who were the husbands in most of these houses, escorting me out when I left, on seeing Prince said Good dog, and made to pat him.

But Prince wasn't a good dog, and instantly showed that he wasn't; whereupon the colonels, recoiling even as I was wont to recoil, asked me, with severity, where I had picked him up.

I hadn't picked him up; he belonged to the house, and went with it when I bought it, I explained.

"Well, I should take care of that dog," the colonels would advise, standing as far back as politeness permitted.

"The idea is he should take care of me," I said.

"I mean, I should beware of him," said the colonels.

But that was precisely what I was already doing. Continually we were growing each more wary of the other. I was nettled by his hostility, I, who had always been such friends with my dogs, and I didn't like the look of him, either; I didn't like his narrow face, and eyes set close together. Nor did I then, and still don't, like black dogs, because of not being able, in the daytime, to see what may be walking about in their coats, and at night not being able, when one lets them out before going to bed, to see where they have got to in the dark.

If you are a careful owner, and yourself let your dog out the last thing, you will not find it much fun standing peering into the dark out of which, should he be a wicked dog like Prince, with no affection nor any sense of duty, he refuses to reappear. Weary of whistling, all

[69]

damp with tepid Devonshire drizzle, I used to stand at the garden door, unprofitably straining my eyes and longing to go to bed. How visible my pale Great Danes used to be, and how easy, when they lingered, which was rare, to go after them! But where, in those dark fields, could I hope to find Prince, black as the night that covered him, and totally invisible from the word go?

Those minutes spent in the doorway, staring out into the wet dark, added each night to my sadness, to the way I missed what I used to have, to the brooding heaviness that oppressed us all in that place—the children, my German maid, and myself equally,—a sadness that seemed to be in the very bricks of the solitary house, set among soppy, flat green fields.

Perhaps it was a house in which people had been unhappy. If so, we carried on the tradition. And each afternoon, looming gigantically through the mists which, that autumn, perpetually enshrouded us, came callers clad in mackintoshes.

§

Autumn, though, doesn't last for ever; nor, as I found out later, does widowhood. Dogs, too, come and go; and before, so it seems, one can turn round, everything that has been has also gone. If it weren't for this, I don't know what we should do, there would be such an accumulation.

So, in due course, did our time in Devonshire end, and it ended, oddly enough, because of Prince. That dog, whom I had never liked and who never liked me, was the real cause of our release from enervation and listlessness to vigour, and renewed appreciation of the happy possibilities of life, though the poor thing paid for it with his own. He took to chasing sheep; and the ultimate effect was to send us rocketing up from the soft hollows of Devonshire, from the veils of mist with callers looming through them, to the hard and brilliant solitude of Swiss mountains.

As long as the sheep weren't there, naturally they couldn't be chased, but one day, after a year of decent black, and a further six months, so as to be well on the side of propriety, of greys and tentative, timid mauves, the seemly inertia in which I had been steeped began to lift, and looking out of my bedroom window at the fields, lush with buttercups but otherwise empty, it being May my sap rose.

"Why not," I thought, burgeoning suddenly into enterprise, "let all this to a farmer, and make a little money?"

I let; the farmer filled the fields with sheep; Prince chased them; and a painful period set in of indignation on one side and concern on the other, of threats and of apologies. But no apologies were of use any more directly that devilish dog not only chased but killed, and I could see for myself that it was bound then to become a case for magistrates and penalties.

Now all persons who have spent much of their time in Germany, and certainly all born Germans, have a great fear of the law. Their one idea is not to attract its attention, to be inconspicuous, to crawl in time, as it were, under tables. Accordingly, when I saw myself within reach of its clutches, even though it was English law and presumably more mild, I began to tremble, while the children, being born Germans, trembled harder, and Elsa the maid, not only born German but of the class which can least easily defend itself, trembled hardest of anybody.

Here indeed was a pretty state of things for a widow, the sole protector of a set of orphans, to have got herself involved in, and all because of a dog she had never liked. From the start I cut a poor figure—anybody who trembles, does,—but I had witnessed the sheep being killed, and had no nerves left.

Haled before a magistrate, the figure I cut continued poor, for, recognising him as one who several times had been to tea, I was inexperienced enough to regard this as a link, and, relieved and reassured, began, out of my turn, to talk.

Instantly I was silenced. I could hardly credit my ears. Incredible that a man who had several times been to tea should silence me; and I stood there outraged, all that was still left in me of *hochgeboren* up in arms, while I listened to him fining me. Why, only a week before, that very man was sitting in my drawing-room being plied with cake. Why, I indignantly remembered, he had actually had three lumps of sugar in every cup. Never again should he hear me offering him another slice of cake. Never again should sugar of mine be lavished on him. He had drunk the last of my cups of tea.

Poor indeed, though, did the figure I cut become when I was informed that Prince was to be handed over to the police to be shot, for on hearing this dreadful sentence, after one gasp of horror, I was sick. Then and there; before everybody; and in spite of the fact that I had never really liked him. But to have to go home, and in cold blood take a poor dog from his dinner, and let him be led away to die . . .

The magistrate, trying to pretend nothing was happening, trying to pretend the room wasn't being rent by unseenly sounds, fixed his eyes on a point well above my convulsed head, and said, "Next case."

PART II

§

DOG IX

Coco

AFTER THIS, I didn't care to stay any longer in that house.
At no time since our arrival in it had I really been happy,
and the circumstances of Prince's end made me quite
sure that what we all wanted was change of air.

I changed the air. Widows are mobile creatures, and
can change any amount of air, choosing where and how
they will live in a way unknown to wives. Irresponsibly
we departed, for the house was still on my hands, and it
is certain that no husband would have countenanced
building a new house—which was what I intended to
do,—before the old one had been got rid of; not, that
is, if one were poor, and we were very nearly poor, or
thought we were. But off I went, trusting to luck that
somebody would come along and buy it; and sure

[77]

enough, hardly were we gone before somebody did. Thus does good fortune follow on the steps of the reckless.

If this were autobiography, I would now describe how I went on being reckless, buying sites in Switzerland which turned out to be impossible because, except beauty, they had nothing,—no roads, no water, none of what must be there if houses are to be built; selling them back to the same people I had bought them from, for half of that which I had paid; engaging an architect on the simple recommendation of a postman I met walking in a lane; behaving altogether as persons do behave who have lately, for the first time in their lives, become completely free, and responsible to no authority of any kind. But it is the story of my dogs. Therefore I will not go into the ups and downs, the joys and fears, the alternating confidence and sinking heart, which were my portion during the year spent building what turned out to be a house of happiness, but proceed straight to Coco.

He was my next dog. A Swiss. Native to the parts we had settled in, and dressed for the cold in the thick coat suitable to those high altitudes—a beautiful coat of wavy brown tipped with silver, which the most spoilt cinema star might have envied. Up the path he came one day to apply for the job of taking care of us—for we were completely isolated, and predominantly female,—and I, seeing him from the window walking so sedately by the side of the peasant accompanying him, so sure of himself, so dignified, composed, beautiful and big, went out to meet him, and he was my dog from that moment to the day of his death.

Except the dogs who are living with me now, I have loved no dog as I loved Coco. His absurd name was the only foolish thing about him. He was so intelligent that to be with him was like being with an unusually delightful companion of one's own species, supposing such a companion could be found who, besides delightful, was entirely devoted, loving and uncritical. He was as useful as he was beautiful, trained to carry parcels carefully, to draw a little cart, to go by himself to fetch the milk each morning, and bring it back without having spilled a drop. Twice a week, too, in the company of the *concierge,* he climbed up the mountain to the nearest village and brought back our provisions and his own, carrying the parcel of raw meat for his dinner in his mouth, and never dreaming, however hungry he might be, of doing anything but take it home to the cook, and wait for it to be presented to him properly, in a dish. Always, indeed, he seemed to behave as if he were conscious of the magnificence of the garment he went about in, and of the necessity of living up, by perfect manners, to his extreme outward splendour. And he knew how much I loved him. I don't believe he could ever have been loved so much before; and this, too, added to his decent, modest pride.

Here he is, the day of his arrival, photographed with

me in the porch; and here he is the following summer, in the position which by that time had become a habit, of lying at my feet whenever I sat down, and putting a protective paw over my ankle:

"*Il ne lui manque que la parole,*" said the *concierge,* who adored him too.

Well, I for one am unable to imagine how anybody who lives with an intelligent and devoted dog can ever be lonely. I had been afraid I might be lonely in that entirely solitary place when the children, after the holidays, went back to school; it was the one doubt I had as to the wisdom of building our nest on a mountain. The house was meant as a holiday home for the children, where they could bring their friends and ski in winter and climb in summer, and I, in between these irradiated periods, was going to work quietly at writing those stories which by now had become our chief support. That had been the idea. But I did wonder secretly, as the first holidays drew to an end, what it was going to be like; I did have doubts, when I saw the last flutter of handkerchiefs from the departing train at the end of September, and turned away to drive up the long winding road home, the endless road, three solid hours of crawl, by myself. After a life spent continually in company, after the tea parties in Devonshire, and the thickly inhabited Schloss in Pomerania, and, before that, my constant Mademoiselle, and, before her, an ubiquitous nurse called, with unaccountable mysteriousness, Da Hooleran—after all these, how was I going to like silence, emptiness, one day succeeding another unmarked by any change, except in the weather and the pudding I had for dinner?

But I had forgotten Coco. There, when I got out of the fly at the point where the road winds off to the village at the top, and one had to take to one's feet for the last bit, he was waiting with the *concierge,* all happy welcome, ready to carry any parcels I might have brought with me; and in the company of that dear dog I walked across the fields of autumn crocuses, through whose translucent petals the setting sun was slanting, reassured and content.

§

October was unbelievably beautiful up there. The weather was perfect, till nearly the end of the month. The great valley below swam in a delicate haze, the brilliant green slopes above were alight with flaming cherry-trees, and the Weisshorn, after Mont Blanc Switzerland's chief pride, towered, glittering and majestic, opposite my bedroom windows.

A peaceful life of routine set in for me, of quiet mornings working undisturbed—for you can't be disturbed if nobody is there except an extremely well-behaved dog,—of meals out in the porch, with the whole of the Simplon range as a finish to the immense picture I could look at between the mouthfuls, of long walks in the afternoons with Coco—*C'est un ours! C'est un ours!* the children would cry who met us,—of evenings spent reading by a wood fire, he stretched out in front of it,

[*83*]

overlapping the rug at each end. Then came a final visit to the terrace before putting him to bed, out from the fire-lit room straight into the vast night, the vast, amazing night, pierced by bright stars, set about with snow-topped mountains, our little house hanging on among them by its eyelashes half-way up to heaven, and, far away beneath us, the lights of the small town in the valley quivering and dancing, as if they were shining through moving water.

Into this majesty, each night Coco and I stepped out before going to bed, and spent a few moments—at least I did, while he sat on his haunches and watched me,—of *recueillement*. This word is as difficult to spell as it is to translate, but it accurately describes the state in which I spent, each night, the last of my waking moments. The *concierge* and his wife, and the *jeune fille,* as they always described the housemaid, were long since asleep, and Coco and I had the whole world, so it seemed in that lofty silence, that unbreathed purity, to ourselves.

Moments of wonder and blessing. And I who had been afraid I might be lonely! Lonely? It was here, in the first complete solitude I had ever known, that I began to suspect that what is called loneliness is what I love best, for how was it possible not to notice that these were the happiest weeks of my life, as far as my life had then got?

Often and often I had had happy ones before, if not uninterruptedly—and who is happy uninterruptedly?— yet in prolonged and very glorious spurts; but there was a quality about this happiness I hadn't till then known, *a something far more deeply interfused,* as Wordsworth put it. Really there is no one like Wordsworth, for describing certain almost indescribable states of mind.

In this condition, then, of enraptured *recueillement,* of fusion with I don't know what of universal and eternal, I spent each night before going to bed, till the snow came. It came quite suddenly. The weather first briefly menaced, and then exploded. Now we shall see, I thought, watching, through the snow-smudged windows, the fury going on outside, now we shall see how much of being alone here I can stand.

But even then, after the first uneasy astonishment at the completeness, during that preliminary blizzard, of our isolation in a house grown suddenly dark, I felt content. For one thing, Coco so obviously enjoyed what was going on. It was what he was used to; it was for precisely this that he had been given his beautiful thick coat; and the *concierge* and his wife, and the *jeune fille,* all being used to it too, if they didn't exactly rejoice during our days of imprisonment they took imprisonment as a matter of course.

"Voilà l'hiver," they informed me, in case I hadn't

noticed it; but we should soon settle down, they added, into *le beau temps* again.

Meanwhile, if it hadn't been for Coco, I daresay after a while I would have found the dark, noisy solitude, when all day and all night the whole universe seemed in a roar, trying; and sometimes during the worst of the gales, crouching by the fire and wondering how long the roof would be able to stand it, I admit that only my hand on his head, and the feel of his kind paw across my foot, gave me courage. Without him, it might well have been that at the end of a few weeks of that sort of thing I might have found myself falling back on fortitude; and therefore I recommend those persons of either sex, but chiefly, it would seem, of mine, whose courage is inclined to fail them if they are long alone, who are rather frightened in the evenings if there is nobody to speak to, who don't like putting out their own lights and climbing silently to a solitary bedroom, who are full of affection and have nothing to fasten it on to, who long to be loved and, for whatever reason, aren't—I would recommend all such to go, say, to Harrods, and buy a dog. There, in eager rows, they will find a choice of friends, only waiting to be given a chance of cheering and protecting. Asking nothing in return, either, and, whatever happens, never going to complain, never going to be cross, never going to judge, and against whom no sin committed will be too great for immediate and joyful forgiveness. Saints, in fact. Cheerful saints, too, which is, I think, important. And numerous, no doubt, as our human saints are, and worthy to be exalted, it would be difficult to find among them a more complete saint than a good dog.

So that, in the words of a poem I came across the other day which gave me great pleasure, I raise

> *my glass to all Good Dogs.*
> *To no particular breed, no special strain*
> *Of certified prize-winners—just to plain,*
> *Unpedigreed Good Dogs . . .*
> *I drink to wagging tails and honest eyes,*
> *To courage, and unguessed-at loyalties*
> *Whose value never will be known or sung.*

§

And one morning I woke up to find *le beau temps* was there again—undeniably *beau,* if different from what I had been basking in before.

There was no room, in this hard-frozen white world, for basking. Now, when we went in and out, Coco and I passed between high banks of snow, beneath icicles hanging, like a fringe of bright spears which every day grew bigger, along the eaves of the house. Now the light was so blinding, blazing downwards from the shining sky and upwards from the shining snow, that I had to wear smoked glasses. Now no paths were anywhere to be seen, and the *concierge,* when he fetched provisions, fetched them on skis. Now in the brief afternoons, instead of going for walks with Coco, I luged, and he, in a frenzy of joy, bounded beside me, kicking up flurries of powdery snow as he ran. Now skirts were impossible and had to be taken off, even the *jeune fille,* on her days out, issuing forth in breeches. Now such an exhilaration of living seized us, that whenever anyone caught anyone else's eye both broke into wide smiles; while as for food, as for the mere act of eating, it became one of the most delightful and important things in the world.

Briefly, we were healthy, and therefore happy, and presumably wise. The sun seemed to pour right through our clarified, accordant bodies. The thin, pure air lifted us along as if we had wings. Indoors we sang, and out of doors we swooped through space on skis and luges. Even the *jeune fille* sang and swooped. Even, more unexpectedly, the grave-faced *concierge,* and his stout wife. When I first saw the stout wife on skis I trembled for her, they were such slender things for the carrying of all that bulk; but off she darted, as sure of herself and them as anybody, disappearing over the lip of the snow like a big, a fat, an unwieldy, but nevertheless a skilled, bird.

'If only, only it will stay like this for the Christmas holidays! If only, only the children are able to share it!' I used to say to myself, I used at last to turn into a sort of prayer.

It did stay like that, and they were able to share it, and I think we would have had the most wonderful Christmas of our lives but for one thing.

That one thing was guests.

§

Guests can be, and often are, delightful, but they should never be allowed to get the upper hand. From now on, till the breaking of the weather in March put an end to their comings and goings—or rather to their comings, for their goings quickly became negligible,— they got the upper hand of me. And in mentioning them I am not giving way to autobiography and for- getting that what I am really writing about is dogs, for it was Coco's attitude to them which causes their ap- pearance in these pages. If I am to write of Coco, I must also write of guests. Otherwise, like so much else, they would have been passed over in silence.

How they got in, to begin with, to my peaceful little house, was this:

I had five children, and each child was to invite, if it chose, two friends out for the Christmas holidays. Such had been my promise in the enthusiastic days when I first began building, and it was still my intention strictly to observe it. But two friends each made ten friends altogether, so that, with my own five, there would be fifteen children staying with me. Wouldn't that be rather much?

Misgivings, as the holidays approached, began to creep round in my mind. Not misgivings that there wouldn't be enough room, because the house had been planned with an eye to the children's probably numerous friends coming out in the holidays. It wasn't this that I was afraid of—it was the number of children, with me the only grown-up.

Soon my apprehensions came in crowds. What if, in that strong, exciting air, the children should become strong and excited too? Fifteen of them, going about being strong and excited, and I the only grown-up. And when the arrivals were actually imminent, imminent to the point of fifteen beds standing ready made, and the first meal, which included a dish of sixty *meringues à la crême,* ordered, I lost my nerve, and by telegram invited a guest of my own. Just to back me up. Just to balance the children's guests.

He was an aged person—rather like Hardy's *Darkling Thrush,* frail, gaunt and small,—picked, from among my friends, for his settled habits. I felt that his mere presence would steady what by this time I was sure was going to be a whooping, hustling crowd of little hooligans. And he arrived. And his habits, within a few hours, became unsettled. And from the first he didn't seem nearly as aged as he had appeared to be down on the flat.

This, I found afterwards, was to be the invariable effect of the house, the surroundings, and the strong air. People came up stiff with years, heavy with experiences, and in a few days had not only forgotten they had ever been through anything or ever had things like rheumatism, but were behaving in a fashion that was really almost regrettably invigorated. The height, the air, the sparkle, produced some strange results. It became, later, a commonplace of life up there that the little wooden house should rock with emotions. Somebody was always having emotions in it—violent ones, because everything in that place was exaggerated. Tears, when they were shed, weren't shed in drops but torrents; admiration was ready and excessive; devotion set in easily, and quickly became extravagant; while as for dislikes, or even hatreds, they were fierce.

I suppose it was because we were all so much invigorated. And I daresay, too, being cut off from the world, and thrown into each other's company as completely as the contents of Noah's Ark when it got stuck on the top of Ararat, had something to do with it. Anyhow, the guests, uncritically pouncing on such material as they found to hand, passionately made the most of it, and in doing so became changed creatures.

My first one, for instance, invited because of his known steadiness, as early as the second day was showing signs of invigoration. These signs appeared first at breakfast, and began with a vehement rubbing of his hands, and a hearty thwacking of the backs of several of the nearest children; and such thwacking being, as I knew, foreign to his nature, I looked on in surprise.

Then, when the children had turbulently rushed from the room, and he and I were alone with the *croissants* and the coffee-pot, he asked me, a note of jovialness with which till then I was unfamiliar in his voice, to tell him, in strict confidence and perfect assurance that it should go no further, who helped me write my stories.

This estranged me. And I was still more estranged by what he said next; for, having inquired what the story I was then writing was about, and I having answered—reluctantly and apologetically, because down on the flat he had seemed so strictly principled,—that I was very sorry but I was afraid it was about adultery, he called out, with horrifying heartiness, "The finest sport in the world!"

What sort of a guest, I asked myself, shocked, was this for a widow, the sole protector of a set of orphans, to have got herself involved in?

But there was worse to come; for quite soon, instead of helping me with the uproarious children, he left off even pretending to be interested in them, and began, to my concern, to concentrate on me. In other words, he left off being just a guest, and turned into a suitor.

I know such subjects are delicate, and if it wasn't for Coco, who encouraged him, I wouldn't touch them. I also know that the high altitude had a lot to do with it. He had never shown the least wish to be a suitor on the flat, but the height went to his head, and perhaps the fact that there was no one else, except children, to speak to. These things are the sport of chance and occasion. A man is persuaded to imagine he likes some particular person by the merest trifle, the merest accident, sometimes, of just place and weather. But the chance and the occasion being present, and the place and the weather being so violently invigorating, he began that which really can only be described as courting, and I, entirely out of sympathy with such rejuvenations, began to evade, to melt away and stay away, while Coco, instead of growling and showing his teeth, was all for it.

I cannot understand Coco. I never did understand Coco in his attitude to suitors. It was impossible that each of them—there were one or two others presently, the conditions being what they were,—it was impossible that each of them should have been the right man for me, and that Coco by instinct should know it. He didn't, as it turned out, by instinct know anything of the kind; he welcomed them all with the same large effusiveness. Odd how that dog seemed to recognise a suitor directly he set eyes on him, picking him out from non-suitors, at whom he didn't so much as glance, and marking him down for immediate attention and encouragement. Long before I had any idea that one was present, and often, I am sure, before the suitor knew it himself, Coco was all over him. I used at last to feel nervous just to see his tail start wagging.

But anyhow, to go back to my first one, he spoiled the Christmas holidays for me, because there is nothing, I suppose, so disconcerting as being stalked when you don't want to be, unless, perhaps, it is not being stalked when you do want to be. A great deal of precious time was spent in evasions, in artfulness, in headings-off,

all of which were made more difficult by Coco, who
fidgeted and at last actually took to whining whenever
he and I were safely in my bedroom, or had escaped
round some unsuspected corner. It soon became evident
that Coco didn't want to escape. His idea seemed to be
that we three ought to hang together; and since it is no
sort of comfort to have a dog who fidgets when he is
alone with one, and no sort of comfort, either, to have a
guest who fidgets when he isn't alone with one, I had a
disappointing time.

The lovely morning he went away, the lovely, happy
morning he went away *unverrichtete Dinge,* as the ex-
pressive German phrase has it, with what recovered joy
did I gaze around me at the works of God! I seemed to
have been separated from them for so long. I seemed to
have been groping about so long among unshared emotions—which is even worse, I think, than groping among
shared ones, though both are apt to be ultimately un-
profitable. There I stood on the terrace, having duly
waved good-bye, and I felt like a convalescent, like one
whose fever has at last left him and who is filled, instead,
by a great peace. The wide valley brimming with light,
the Weisshorn, and Rothorn, and Simplon range en-
circling it in a ring of radiance, had never been more
beautiful. A new freshness was in the air, a new purity.
It might have been the first morning in Eden, so fair

and stainless was it. Behind me the windows of the house were all flung open, and at one of them the *jeune fille* was vigorously singing, while she banged the bedding of him who had just gone. Out from the kitchen poured a gorgeous smell of stew being cooked for a picnic—he had declined picnics,—and when it was ready Coco, restored to his real self, would help me carry the bucket, filled with brimming lusciousness, to the spot the children and I were going to eat in, up on the snow-slopes, sitting on our luges in the sun.

Darling children. Dear dog. Precious freedom. Adorable world.

Such was the effect on me of my first guest's departure.

§

But I would not have it thought that I am churlish. I like to believe my impulses are all towards hospitality. Certainly I ordered the dinners while he was there with much care, and brought out my bottles of wine so diligently that at last there were none left, and we had to relapse into lemonade. But when things leave off there is generally, I think, a feeling of relief. However pleasant they may have been while they lasted, it is pleasant, too, to relax, to drop back into one's carpet-slippered normal. Especially this is true when it is a suitor who leaves off, for suitors are, after all, a strain. Even if they are the sort one turns a deaf ear to, one does, so long as they are about, give one's whiskers, as it were, an extra twist, and this means effort, and effort means time.

I had grudged the effort; I had grudged the time; and each night when I went to bed I had grudged, thinking them over, the pains I had taken to look, at dinner, what I hoped was my best. Yet the effort had been made, the time spent, and the shameful pains taken. What old Eve, I wondered, was this coming out in me?

Fortunately I am not writing autobiography, so that I needn't go into that.

§

Presently, the holidays being over, Coco and I were alone again, and once more took up life together with what certainly was gusto on my part, and looked like gusto on his.

I say looked like gusto, because, though no dog could seem more delighted to have me all to himself, yet there were moments when I caught him sniffing at the door of the room which had been my late guest's. And he sniffed with a melancholy air. And when I called him away, came reluctantly.

Had there, I began to wonder, been something outstandingly admirable about that man, and just the sort of thing Coco knew I would like? They say dogs always know; and I was inclined to believe it, and vaguely dallied with the not unpleasurable notion that I had probably missed a good husband, till more guests ascended on me, and from the way Coco immediately dashed at certain among them, picking them out at once for almost overwhelming attentions, I knew there could be no truth in the saying. Everybody couldn't possess just the sort of qualities I would like. Dogs didn't know. Dogs made grotesque mistakes. It was simply an affair of altitude and cut-offness that guests should develop this tendency to do that which, if there were a verb corresponding to the substantive suitor, such a verb would express.

These new guests had come upon me because I am never able to say no,—not quickly, that is, not at the precise, the critical moment. Give me time, and I can say it with any woman, but telephone to me and I will agree to everything.

They telephoned to me; and as a result they almost immediately became guests. It appeared they had met my late one at Geneva, whither he had gone on leaving me, and Geneva being a flat place, disposed as it is about the edges of a lake, he had soon, it seemed, recovered there from the heady sparkle of my mountains, and now was seeing things in their true proportions.

These true proportions had no doubt led him to recognise that he had had the escape of his life, and in his thankfulness there was no praise high enough for my house and everything in it. I was, it appeared he had informed my friends—if those can be called friends whom one has occasionally met in London,—the perfect hostess. There was an enchantingly, an almost misleadingly, friendly dog. The servants were most quaint. The food quite extraordinary. In fact, it was a place which should certainly be visited if one were at all run down, or at all getting older.

Spellbound at the other end of the telephone, I listened to these encomiums. It being a telephone, I wasn't calm enough to dissect them then and there. When I did later, I couldn't help suspecting them. That bit about the food, for instance, and the misleading dog. Was he, then, far from heaping coals of fire on my head as I had first thought, just being vengeful? It certainly looked like vengefulness, to land me with four more guests.

Meanwhile, on the telephone, these guests, not guests

then but soon to become so, having explained that they were inclined to be run down and that one of them, at least, was getting older, I was agreeing to everything. They planned, they said, to spend the rest of the winter in Rome, and thought it would be so nice to break their journey at my station in the valley, and come up and see me. Come up to lunch, perhaps. Or, if it were too far for that, perhaps for a night. Or even, one night more not making much difference, for a wonderful week-end. To all of which, such being my nature when faced by telephones, I heard myself saying enthusiastically, "Oh, but what *fun!*"

So they broke their journey three hours from Geneva, and arrived on my doorstep in a clump. Why they arrived in a clump was because they were a family—a mother, a daughter, and two sons; and Coco, I was perturbed to see, immediately dashed welcomingly at the two sons.

Now began, not a week-end, for, once arrived, they stayed, but whole weeks of a life at variance with the calm majesty of our surroundings. There were the mountains all round us, setting us an example of noble untroubledness, and we didn't take the slightest notice. My little house seethed. The mother, who was the one getting older, at once began, rather frighteningly, to get younger. The daughter, who was the one inclined to be run down, was in tearing spirits by breakfast the next morning. The two sons, unfortunately of the age, as Coco had instantly found out, which likes older women, lost no time, there being nobody else at hand, in devoting themselves to me. They rushed to pick up things I dropped. They snatched that from me which I still held. They vied with each other in reading poetry to me in sheltered corners. They hung on my words, and laughed appreciatively every time I opened my mouth —sometimes even before I had opened it, which is conduct that easily dries up the springs of conversation.

Such young men do exist, and it is a pity, because they are so bad for the older women, who give heed to their flutings at their own peril. I daresay they would have been bad for me too if I had taken them seriously, but I wasn't quite old enough to do that, and my sole reaction to their devotion was that I was irked.

I was, indeed, much irked. It irked me to find that, though on the level of the house they merely smouldered, take them for a climb another five hundred feet up, and they erupted. It irked me to observe the mother and sister presently becoming watchful; and it irked me perhaps most of all to see Coco's behaviour, to see his barefaced attempts to promote *tête-à-têtes*.

He had an embarrassing habit of running from me to the young men, and from the young men back again to me, violently wagging his tail, looking up eagerly into our faces, barking if we took no notice, and actually going so far as to pull at our sleeves. And the mother would say, "What a strange dog that is. One would almost think——"

But she broke off. By the second week of their visit we were constantly, in conversation, breaking off.

§

I would have all couples neatly paired in years, the forties with the forties, and the twenties with the twenties. Should the forties, as sometimes happens, not care about other forties, and wish to frequent twenties, in their own interests they should be discouraged, and equally those twenties should be discouraged who, with the inexperience of their age, suppose they could be lastingly happy with forties.

Fortunately in my house there wasn't, at that time, anybody disposed to listen to the siren pipings of youth, and one would have thought that we all, in consequence, might have been quite happy together. But we weren't. I think it was because we were too healthy. Extreme physical well-being does easily bring with it mental upheavals; bursting with vigour, one needs must, it seems, either love or fight. My new guests, owing to the conditions prevailing, having nobody to love began to fight, and nothing ever being done up there by halves, after vehemently enjoying themselves the first few days they began with equal vehemence not to—the sons because all Coco's efforts to bring them and me together only succeeded in widening what rapidly became a rift between us, the mother and daughter because they felt the rift and didn't like it, though they would have liked it still less if it hadn't been there.

These exasperations, however, didn't make them go. On the contrary, they made them stay; for there had developed in them that tendency to have things out which is bound, sooner or later, to appear in the super-vigorous who can't get away from each other, and till they had had things out they plainly weren't going to move on to Rome. The mother wanted to have things out with the sons, and the daughter with her brothers. They all, I feared, wanted to have things out with me, for I couldn't help knowing that one of the reasons for their desire to give and receive explanations was myself. Not the only reason, but one of them. There were others, such as railway-tickets. In that intoxicating air almost anything did to rouse passions, and I would not rate myself too highly. The only difference between me and the tickets was that they were discussed openly, and I wasn't. To discuss me, bedrooms were gone into, and doors shut; and I, left alone in the hall after tea—nothing used to happen during the day, because we were active out of doors, besides being separated by skis,—I, then, left alone in the hall with Coco, and knowing what was going on upstairs, was irked.

"Gerald, come to my room a minute. I want to show you something," the mother would say; and soon the daughter would take the other brother away, making the same remark, except that he was Gilbert. And the house being of wood, and the floors thin, I sometimes, sitting quietly by the fire alone with Coco, wasn't able not to hear their louder conversations, such as, *Five children,* or—particularly nettling, for it wasn't yet true,— *She must be forty if she's a day.*

Then I would get up, fetch my fur coat from its peg, ostentatiously whistle for Coco, and go out with him into the night, passing through the little fir wood behind the house, across the crackling snow to a rock I knew; and there I would sit and watch the stars coming out in the pale green sky, and take comfort from the immense indifference and silence.

Plainness and clearness without shadow of stain,
Clearness divine—

I would murmur. Yes; that was what one needed, I said to myself, continuing nettled, but beginning to be rather ashamed of it in that icy purity, that frozen stillness, with all the little streams of summer smitten soundless among their rocks.

Out would come another star, winking at me over the white shoulder of the Rothorn. Round me stood the mountains, exquisite examples of peace—

A world above man's head, to let him see
How boundless might his soul's horizons be—

and here was I, minding because guests went into their bedrooms and told each other I had five children. Well, so I had. Nothing could possibly be more true.

How vast, yet of what clear transparency—

and minding because they said I was forty, which I certainly would be some day, if I went on living at the rate I was doing.

How it were good to abide there and be free—

The fact was, I reflected, my eyes on the glittering slopes of the Weisshorn, we were all too close together, and my guests, being of one family, only made this closeness worse. The remedy—it burst upon me suddenly in a flash,—was not to waste my serenity vainly longing for the guests I had to go, but to invite yet more of them. Unrelated ones. Guests of another blood. And for the first time I perceived that if you wish to be free, while still remaining hospitable, it isn't a few guests you want, it is many. Fling your doors wide. Fill your house to the brim. Then they will be so busy with each other that they will have no time for you, and you can get on in peace with your next book.

At this I rose to my feet—

> *How fair a lot to fill*
> *Is left to each man still!*

I observed, triumphantly addressing the solemn mountains; and hurrying with Coco back to the house, at once began writing letters and sending telegrams.

§

This not being autobiography, I needn't go much into what happened next, because all Coco did for the next few weeks—and it is about him, really, that I am writing,—was to yawn. Enough, therefore, to say that, having provided the young men with suitable girls, and the sister with somebody who wasn't her brother, and the mother with somebody else's father, everybody behaved as I had hoped, except the father.

About him I had, it seemed, erred; for having led him to her who was, I had supposed, his natural complement, he showed little desire to settle down with her, and soon, looking out of the window, said that he thought he would go and stretch his legs a bit, and disappeared after the girls.

It upset all my plans, his doing this. The mother had strained a tendon ski-ing, and was obliged to stay indoors for a day or two resting it, and it had been my idea that he, a man well on in the sixties, would like to keep her company and sit quiet and chat. Which would set me free.

But I had forgotten the invigorating air. Also, he was of those who don't like their contemporaries, especially not contemporaries who are bandaged. The mother, necessarily, was bandaged, with a foot for the moment *hors de combat* and hoisted high on the cushions of the sofa on which she was forced to lie. But what is a foot, compared to the rest of one? Nothing that had happened to her out ski-ing interfered with her mental responsiveness. Her soul, her spirit, all those parts of a human being which are justly valued as precious, were as ready to make contacts as ever. I'm afraid my new

[*107*]

guest laid no store by that sort of contact. He didn't want mental responsiveness. What he liked was youth, and after it he barefacedly went—spoiling, the girls told me later, their climbing parties, because, invigorated as he might be, he yet was older than they were, and lagged going up the mountain and lamented coming down it.

The result of his not wanting to stay at home with fogies—I believe that man regarded both the mother and myself as fogies, and of course compared to the girls, who all were under twenty, it is possible that we may very nearly have seemed so, hard as it is to face,—the result of his not wanting to stay with persons of this description, was that nobody was left to keep my lamed guest company but me.

This was as unexpected as it was unfortunate. Instead of being freer for having invited more guests, I was less free. But what could I do? Humaneness, as well as hospitality, demanded that I should not leave one who was stricken. So there I sat, hour after endless hour, preserving, I hope, a bland exterior, while my thoughts despairingly hovered round all that I might else so happily have been doing.

With us sat Coco, and yawned. He had lost interest in the two sons since they had lost interest in me, and had from the first taken none in either of the other male guests. Now he was bored. He couldn't make out why he should have to sit indoors on such fine mornings, and why I wasn't out as usual on skis, with him dashing along beside me down the slopes. Incessantly, enormously, he yawned, his great head thrown back and cleft redly in two, making all the noises old men make who yawn, and are past caring what anybody thinks of them.

That dog was the most amazing yawner I have ever met. Impossible not to catch it from him, and accordingly there were three of us yawning. At first they were ladylike, suppressed yawns, quite different from Coco's shameless abandonments, and the mother would put her hand nicely in front of her face each time, and when she had finished say apologetically, "Really, I don't know what has come over me this morning." But, after a bit, she just yawned. Openly, at last, we both did, with no sort of attempt at disguise.

And that was another curious effect of living so high up: we lost our decencies. Not, I naturally don't mean, our major decencies, for from those only death would have separated us, but all the minor ones went. This open yawning, without at last a hand or anything hiding it, is an instance. And there were other instances I might give, if I were writing autobiography; but, perhaps fortunately, as I am not, I needn't.

§

It wasn't till the beginning of March that the fine weather in the mountains broke, and the whole time it went on so did my guests. Not the same ones, but one guest, as I had already learned, leads to another; and back in their offices or their cathedrals—for ten days I had harboured a prebendary,—back, I say, in the places whence they had come, and conspicuous by their sunburn among the pale crowds of England, my late guests enthusiastically described what they had been doing, and the mouths of those who listened watered.

I know, from the results, that this was so. More acquaintances wrote touching letters, saying how much they longed for air that was pure, how much they envied me mine, and how wretched it was to be so utterly broke that they couldn't manage St. Moritz that year. And since, as I have already indicated, I am not able to say No when taken suddenly, nor, I find, if appeals are made to my goodnature—it is so flattering to be supposed goodnatured!—I wrote back in each case and said, Do come. Besides, I did feel that to have that roomy châlet, and all its bathrooms, in such persistently crystalline weather only for me and Coco, while people in

[*110*]

London were being swamped by rain or strangled by fogs, was in the nature of a disgrace.

Accordingly my house was never empty. On the contrary, since few went and many came, it ended by being full to overflowing, and, except that there were no bills at the end, very like an hotel. A popular resort, in fact. If I had been in Baedeker, I daresay I would have got three stars.

Three stars, though, or that which they represent, are expensive, and presently I found that I was growing poor. I had started off on my career as hostess—a career quite new to me, for in Pomerania we had no guests,— in a spirit of uncalculating light-heartedness. If I thought at all, I supposed, largely, that what is enough for one is enough for two, and that the more people you feed the less it costs. These suppositions were erroneous. They might be truths for an hotel-keeper, and certainly hotels do seem able to take one in for less in proportion, so to speak, as one is more, but they are not truths for such as myself. And discovering this I became, at intervals, pensive.

On Saturdays, when I paid the week's bills, I was pensive to the point of not being able, in conversation with my guests at meals, to show any of what is best described as *verve,* and this, I knew, was to be lamented. A hostess, if she is to do her duty satisfactorily by her

guests, should be in a constant condition of *verve*. When
she is with them, at least, this should be her condition.
Let her droop, if droop she must, in her bedroom, but in
their presence let there unflaggingly be *verve*.

On Saturdays I had no *verve*. I sat at the head of my
table emptied of everything except uneasiness, the eye
that still had hospitality in it—more and more did I re-
semble Mrs. Todgers,—glazed, and the one that had cal-
culation shining unnaturally. How long, I asked myself,
would I be able to go on providing, with any sort of
decent lavishness, puddings? How long before the meals
would have to end, abruptly and ignominiously, in just
nuts? And those maids—some of my guests, who needed
more careful putting together, brought their maids,—
were uncontrollable creatures, it appeared, in the
kitchen, meek as they might seem when I came across
them in passages pressing themselves politely against
the wall. And that detective—one of my guests was
obliged by his government to have a detective hanging
round him wherever he went, for it was early 1914, and
the suffragettes were after him,—judging from the bills,
he made really dreadful holes in the whisky.

Pensive, on those Saturdays, I therefore sat, unable
to keep up even a pretence of *verve;* and I don't know
what would have happened, to what petty curtailment
of comfort I wouldn't in my uneasiness have descended,

or to what heights of simple frankness I might not, for the same reason, have ascended, explaining to my guests that it would be well if they were to go away now, and leave me to finish another book, if my attention hadn't been switched off on to something quite different.

This something was a new guest. He hadn't been invited, but, on some pretext which I afterwards perceived to have been thin, just came.

One would have thought that being so much worried about puddings and all, I had enough to do looking after the guests I had already, without taking on another one. And so I had, but this one was different; for this one, climbing slowly up the ice-covered path to my front door, and slipping back a step in every two, wasn't so much another guest as Doom. And from one's doom there is no escape.

§

I don't know that doom is a very nice word. It does suggest, I think, shuddering and cold sweat. There was none of that, though, about Coco's welcome to it when it opened my front door and walked in, nor can it be fairly said that there was any of it about mine. True I had a feeling, unusual so soon after breakfast, that I was in the hands of God, but otherwise I wasn't aware of any particular discomfort. Nor did I remember, till later, that the only other time in my life I had had this feeling was when I was dressing to go to the party in Italy at which I met my first husband. It is a sinking feeling. Perhaps husbands have never altogether agreed with me.

Sitting, then, behind a pile of household books, for it was Saturday, I was alone with Coco, who was yawning. He knew these mornings, and disliked them as much as I did. The others had all gone off into the sun with food and skis, and wouldn't be back till dusk. It seemed to him hard, I could see by his expression, as he sat opposite me on his resigned haunches and yawned in my face, that he and I should be shut up indoors on such a brilliant winter day. But he didn't know how near excitement was. Till the steps that were slithering every minute closer had rounded the shoulder of the mountain, even he couldn't hear them, and it was only when they began to climb the slope to the house that he broke off in the middle of a yawn, pricked up his ears, became taut with attention, and then rushed to the door. What he was listening to, what he was rushing to meet, was approaching Doom. Mine, and, indirectly, his.

The door opened straight from the porch into the

living-room where, heated by pipes as well as a huge log fire, we spent most of our time, and Coco, after sniffing rapturously at the crack along its bottom, broke into a series of short, jubilant barks. I knew those barks. I also knew the peculiar ecstasy of his tail. Everything he was doing was by now familiar to me; and I was forced to conclude that somewhere, quite near, must be another suitor.

Supine I sat, watching Coco. Another suitor. There hadn't been one since the prebendary, and I had supposed them to be over. There does come a moment, I had said to myself, not sure whether I was pleased or not, when suitors are over, and perhaps it wasn't a new one arriving, but my first one of all come back, the one I had invited to help me with the children at Christmas. Come back to see how I was getting on. Come back, it might be, to inquire whether I had liked the four guests he had sent me, and have the laugh of me.

In this, however, I did him an injustice. He was a much nicer man than that. Directly he had got over any little anger he may have felt, and any small desire to get even with me, he wouldn't, I knew really in my heart, be petty, and it turned out to be true that wherever he was at that moment, in Geneva still or back in England, he certainly wasn't climbing up the snow-slippery path to my front door.

Somebody was, though. Even I could hear that somebody was, and somebody who roused wilder expectations in Coco than any I had yet seen. Why? I wondered, my hands folded, my head meek, my whole attitude unconsciously receptive of, and resigned to, Doom.

The answer, though only Coco then knew it, was that this wasn't an ordinary suitor, flickering first, then flaring, and finally fizzling out for want of stoking, but one who would presently become a husband; and on the door being opened and a head put in, he rushed to give him the welcome suitable to so important an arrival.

He was, in fact, all over him. "Come in, come in— oh, *do* come in! This is our house, but from now on it is yours and everything in it," he seemed to be passionately conveying by leaps, licks, waggings, and loud, glad yelps.

As for me, I didn't move. I was too heavy with that strange sense of God's hands to do anything but sit still. And the new arrival said, mopping his brow with one hand, and holding the excited Coco off with the other, "You should have your path done."

And I said, motionless in my chair, hardly turning my bowed head, already sunk in acquiescence, "My path?"

And he said, "Cinders. That's what you must put down."

[*116*]

§

Such were his first words. Looking back, I recognize them as characteristic; but as this isn't autobiography, I needn't go into that. All I need explain is that he was a man I had met once or twice in London while I was building my mountain home, and, being apt to issue immensely cordial invitations when their materialisation seems remote, I had suggested, no doubt with every appearance of warmth, that he should come and stay in it as soon as it was finished.

Now it was finished, and he had come—looked in, he said, on his way to I forget where. But my house wasn't on the way to anywhere, and presently it appeared that he knew it wasn't, and that his luggage was waiting in a sledge round the corner, just in case, he said jovially, proceeding with his well-laid plan, I should ask him to stay. For he had a plan, he told me afterwards, and was as aware as Coco that he was a suitor. What he didn't yet know, and Coco did, was that from a suitor he would presently proceed to be a husband. This—it seems strange to think there was anything that should have,— depended, however, on me, and I, filled with a highly handicapping sense of inevitability, of being predestined,

[*117*]

without a struggle walked into the preliminaries of its accomplishment.

"But of course you must stay," I said with fatal hospitality, unconsciously taking the first step.

He wore goloshed, cloth-sided boots into which the tops of his trousers were tucked, and a starched white collar. Across his waistcoat was a gold watch-chain. He didn't look like a man meant for mountains, or who had any intention of going up them. If he stayed, it was even then plain that he would stay indoors. Perhaps a turn or two on the terrace in the sun occasionally, but chiefly he would sit indoors. And I would sit with him. And together, in a sitting position, though neither of us yet knew it, we would advance towards both our Dooms.

§

The house was now very nearly full. It was quite full of emotions, for added to those already prevailing were the ones that developed in him who had just joined us. At that time things weren't going too well with the pairings-off. They had become mixed up, and infidelities, I gathered, were taking place. These are usually attended by discomfort for somebody, and in that high, strong air discomfort easily became rages. Half my guests, accordingly, were raging, most of the others seemed distracted and uncertain, while only a few went about looking smug.

It was pleasant, then, to have someone arrive who knew nothing of the local agitations, and sat smoking his pipe unruffled and unconcerned, beaming round at everybody while he bided his time. I didn't know that what he was doing was biding his time; I merely thought him, in that unsteady atmosphere, refreshingly rocklike. A restful man, I said to myself; a reliable, kind, simple, restful man. And so sensible, too, about those cinders— for I had done as he directed, and the path to the house was now black instead of white, and, though it didn't look at all nice, it was a comfort to know that he could go up and down it without slipping.

Gradually it became my chief concern that he shouldn't slip, that he should be safe and comfortable out of doors as well as in, that he should have the chair he liked, that the meals should be according to his wishes, which turned out to be chiefly legs of mutton. I can't account for my behaviour. I had never before felt any desire to serve, to obey, to stand with bowed head and hands folded, to be, as it were, the handmaid of the lord. But from the first I was meek and pliable, giving in without a struggle, overcome by that strange sensation of God's hands.

The other guests looked on in surprise. Obviously I was being courted, and equally obviously was doing nothing to stop it. Not thus had I behaved to the prebendary when he, too, was courting. Him I had resisted, while now I was as wax. For him no cinders had been laid down, nor heed given to his favourite dishes. Silent he had sat in the evenings, pretending to read *Hibbert's Journal,* while I, at the farther end of the room, was being self-consciously vivacious with others.

Now, how much changed was my behaviour, and how natural that those guests who had lived through the prebendary should observe this change with interest. They took to leaving me and the new arrival alone, after a fashion only to be described as marked. If they opened a door and found us there, they hastily shut it and went away. Apart we sat, with Coco very proud and happy between us, and in the evenings, when the living-room had perforce to be invaded, the others tactfully huddled in the most distant corners.

"Do you see how they feel you belong to me?" my suitor would say; adding in the same breath, for he was one who thought most things of equal importance, his hand on Coco's head, "You should give this dog horsemeat, chopped up raw."

"Plainness and clearness without shadow of stain"—I would once again murmur at this; but in how different

a context. And began, ominously, to tell myself that a widow was only half a woman.

§

At this point, if I weren't writing about dogs, I might say a few words about widows. Many are the reflections they have given rise to in my mind since once more I became one. There is nothing I don't now know about them; and the thing I know most clearly is that, far from being half a woman, a widow is the only complete example of her sex. In fact, the finished article.

But dogs are my subject, and to dogs I will return—to Coco, the dog of this particular period, except for whose behaviour in connection with them, the preliminaries to my second marriage would have been passed over in silence. I cannot, though, pass over them in silence when that dog made such a noise. His exuberant delight filled the house. Almost it seemed as if he had been feeling the responsibility of taking care of me single-handed, and was overjoyed that somebody should be going to share it with him. Anyhow he behaved as if this were so, and it never appeared to occur to him that he and I were very well as we were.

I must say it sometimes occurred to me—in the

[*121*]

watches of the night, for instance, when, released from the pressure of constant company, I was better able to think. Then that sinking feeling would come over me again, and was only to be got rid of by my remembering Coco's enthusiasm. "Dogs always know," I assured my uneasy mind—choosing to forget how little this dog had really known on other occasions, for one needs must somehow buoy oneself up. Perhaps, though, it isn't a very good sign when those considering marriage feel they need buoying.

With hardly any hesitation, then, I advanced towards, let us say, my destiny, for really I don't think doom is a very nice word. By the time the weather broke, and the guests, including my suitor, fled like leaves scurrying before the gale to the valley and the reassuring shelter of trains, I was well within its clutches—or let us say its circumjacence, for I don't think clutches is a very nice word either. Yet even so, acquiescent as I was in the position I had got into, there was enormous relief at being alone again, a long drawing of the breath, a sensation of something for a while, at least, put off—the word *escaped* not having yet occurred to me.

From the wind-swept terrace Coco and I watched the guests, including my suitor, go, Coco's ears blown straight up into the air, and the ends of my woollen scarf

wildly flapping. I daresay our two figures looked forlorn
enough, that grey morning, to those departing down the
path. Behind us was the empty house, behind that the
melancholy flank of a rocky mountainside in bad
weather, above were the driving clouds, and all round
trees were straining and rocking. Yes; a forlorn pair we
must have looked, and I could imagine my late guests
thinking, "Poor little thing."

How wrong they were. I wasn't a poor little thing at
all. Even as early as this, such is the relief when pressure
is removed, even in the very act of waving my last good-
byes, I found it quite difficult to pull a suitably regretful
face, and I know I went back into the house, the silent
house, the deliciously empty house, with steps so brisk
that they nearly ran.

The fact is, and it is no good denying it, gaps are
pleasant. Any gaps. And the gap a lover leaves is sometimes the most pleasant of all. One badly needs, after
his or other prolonged company, but especially after
his, to be restored and renewed, and it can only be done
really properly in a gap. Therefore I couldn't help welcoming this one as blessed. My heart grew light. So long
submerged, I had the sensation of at last coming up to
the surface. So long flattened, I seemed at last to be ex-
panding to my normal size. And the first thing I did on
going into the empty, roomy house, was to ring the bell,

[*123*]

tell the *jeune fille* to finish the current leg of mutton in the kitchen, and order a poached egg for my dinner.

§

These are agreeable sensations; but they are not the sensations she should have who is considering marrying again. Gradually it became clear to me that they were not, and that the satisfaction I felt at being alone was a sign, surely, that having become a widow I ought to stay one. Else why, after the first natural relief which, I insist, follows *any* departure, did I not miss my suitor more? That couldn't be love, which found so deep a contentment in the lover's absence. I suspected it then but I know it now, for there have been times since in my life when I have missed people so extravagantly that I couldn't keep away even from the place their coats had hung in, and would go and stroke the very hook on which they had been accustomed to keep their hats. There I would stand, clinging to the indifferent hook, forlornly counting, as I did so, hours, days, weeks in a fashion which will be familiar to the bereft. *This time yesterday we were still together . . . this time last week . . . this time a month ago. . . .* That sort of thing.

But now it was only Coco who paid memorial visits,

sniffing where coats had been, scratching at the door of the room my suitor had slept in, while I, back at work again, and daily more filled with that sense of harmony, of inner balance, which being at work has always given me, was quickly reaching the stage of marvelling that I should have so much as thought of further husbands. What on earth did I, of all people, want with a lot of husbands? I asked myself in wonder. Besides, by steadily sticking to poached eggs for dinner I was getting well abreast of my expenses, and the bills of Saturdays held no more terrors for me. Also, in a few weeks Easter would be there, and the fine weather, and holidays, and happy children; so that life every minute seemed to grow more delightful.

> *How fair a lot to fill*
> *Is left to each man still!*

Yes, indeed.

Then one evening, fingering the bookshelves, I chanced to take down a volume of Goethe, and opening it happened to light on his great declaration that *im Wahren, Guten, Schönen resolut zu leben* was the one line worth taking.

That settled it. The bare words filled me with a strange rapture. So would I live, a dedicated widow,— a widow, I vowed, holding the book tight to my breast,

[*125*]

mindful of her past blessings, and of all the kindness and indulgence she had received in her far-off
Pomeranian home, a widow intent only on raising a
worthy monument to him she had lost, by following,
with all her heart, the advice of his great countryman.

Clearly this didn't include another husband, for who
can raise a monument to one while turning over the
idea of taking on another? Such conduct would at least
be tactless, and probably something much worse; therefore, before beginning to raise, to build, to consecrate, I
thought I ought to write to my suitor and explain.

I did so that very night. By this time I had had several
letters from him, each breathing the calm assurance, the
placid taking for granted, which had so much helped
to reduce me to subservient acquiescence when he was
actually present, and I had answered them evasively,
chiefly with descriptions of the weather. Now, though,
if I intended to follow in Goethe's magnificent steps,
evidently the first thing I had to do was to be *resolut*
with my suitor, and I wrote and told him, as nicely as
possible, that on the whole I rather felt—it is politeness
which makes one seem less firm than one really is,—
that once a widow always a widow ought to be my
motto, suspecting, as I did, that I had no real gift for the
married state, or, more precisely, for repetitions of the
married state, and that, by and large, and looking at it

all round and taking one thing with another, I did think it generally best, after a certain age, to leave well alone.

By return I got a letter asking me to define the word Well.

I couldn't. At no time have I been much good at defining, and to try to do so in this case would have involved me, I perceived, in a slur on the memory of him I had lost; so, leaving the question of widows aside, I wrote and told him about Goethe, and the line of life recommended by that great and wise man, a line which, anyhow for me, didn't include more husbands.

Anxious to make myself clear, and warming to my work, I explained that no two people would probably want to be *resolut* about the same thing at the same moment—what would seem *Wahr* and *Gut* and *Schön* to one of them, mightn't seem at all *Wahr* and *Gut* and *Schön* to the other, especially if the other hadn't slept, or hadn't liked his dinner. But the mere word *resolut*, I said, had put strength into me like a transfusion of blood, and now I saw plainly where true joys were to be found, and that the *Wahr* for me was work, and the *Gut* was my children, and the *Schön* was in resolutely devoting myself to these things. I hoped, I said, that he would wish me luck, just as I wished him luck. I wished him, I said, every possible happiness, with somebody far more worthy than I was. And I finished up by signing myself his true friend, who would always remember him with sincerest goodwill and affection.

It was a beautiful letter, I thought. The only thing I left out was offering to be a sister to him, because it didn't happen, at the moment, to occur to me. But even as it was, I thought it a beautiful letter, and I must say I was surprised and hurt when all I got back was a postcard.

When I came to London, the postcard briefly stated, we would talk things over.

When I came to London? But I wasn't going to London, I answered—also on a postcard, for two, I said to myself with just indignation, can write postcards.

Then there was silence. *Well,* I thought, as the days passed, Coco fetched the letters, and never, in the bag, was one from him I had supposed adored me. At first I was afraid this meant there was going to be a surprise visit of expostulation, and agitatedly I considered where, in such an event, I could hide. But I needn't have troubled; nothing happened; he neither came nor wrote.

Later I discovered that he was biding his time, and that he could bide any amount of time to get what he wanted; but not knowing this then, and being as desirous as most women of eating my cake and having it too, I was first surprised, then indignant, and finally aggrieved. That long, that affectionate, that kind, that beautiful letter of mine, to be answered only by a post-card! True I had wanted to finish the business, but I hadn't wanted to finish it like this. And a feeling of desolation gradually came over me, of being deserted on a dark howling mountain, with nobody anywhere in the whole world really loving me. And presently I took to going to the place his coat used to hang in—though only, I told myself, to call Coco out of it, and scold him for a silly dog.

§

At the end of March, at the very tip-over into April, the storms at last began to slow down, and we found the first violet.

I say we, for if Coco took no more notice of it than Peter Bell of primroses, it was yet he who, excitedly fol-lowing some private interest of his own, drew me on towards the rock I used to sit on in the winter when flee-ing from the mother, the daughter, and the two sons; and there, stretching its little neck out beneath the rock and peeping at the sun, was a violet.

This was an event. Even as the twig of olive in the dove's beak was to Noah, so was that first violet to me. It was assurance. It was hope. The winter was over and

[*129*]

gone. Darkness was done with. The last vestiges of snow, still lurking in cold corners, would soon disappear, and nothing but light and loveliness was ahead for months on end.

Down I sat by that blessed little flower, and would have liked to hug it; and I daresay those who live within hail of hothouses, or have florists' shops round the corner, will think this foolish, but I can assure them it wasn't, for what I felt was a most noble rapture, leading me straight to the making of fresh vows. Just as the violet stretched out to the sun, so would I stretch out towards a future that should shine only with things lovely and of good report, towards that *resolut leben* which had, for a brief and shameful period, been inclined to wobble; because, by the time I reached this memorable moment of return of light after darkness, of spring after winter, I was quite normal again, and so was Coco, and both of us had long left off any melancholy memorial sniffings.

Here, then, was life before me cleared of lumber, ready for the next act, and bright with a sense of escape. Now I knew what the feeling had been the morning my suitor left—it wasn't a feeling of temporary putting off, as I had then supposed, but of downright, simple escape, of the escape of a soul like a bird from the net of the fowler; and the days flew by harmonious with work, happy with the knowledge that each of them brought the holidays nearer, and those dear children on whom my thoughts could now rest again, free from the prickings of conscience which had disturbed them while I was lending an ear to the blandishments of courtship and saying silly things to myself about a widow being only half a woman.

Half a woman? No one could feel less like half of anything than I when I found the violet and praised God; or when, a week later, entirely filled and rounded out with single-minded mother-love, I joyously went down to the station in the valley to meet my little flock, and bring it up safe to the house which, from thenceforward, was to be devoted only to its welfare and happiness.

Thenceforward. I sigh and I smile now, so long afterwards—ultimately, perhaps, one will always be able to smile,—remembering this confident *thenceforward*. There was to be no thenceforward of that kind beyond just those holidays. Coco would not again meet us at the place we got out at, eager to carry any loose parcels, barking his welcome long before our crawling carriage had turned the final bend. That rapturous Easter homecoming, with all of us talking at once at the tops of our voices as we crossed the fields, picking our way between patches of half-melted snow, a child hanging on each of my arms, the others pressing as near as they could, and a proud dog walking importantly ahead with the most precious of the handbags in his mouth, was not to be repeated. Fortunate, then, this being so, that we should have crammed the last holidays so full of happiness, that we hadn't cared that it should be so cold and the frost not yet out of the ground and the winter keeping on blustering back in snow flurries, nor that, in spite of its being Easter, and in spite of its being April, there should be no leaves.

What did this matter to us? Why should we, who were so glad to be together again, mind about things like leaves? As though the place had been alive with leaves, we had our meals out of doors, obstinately behaving as if it were real spring, and only laughing when a boisterous and nipping wind snatched our table-napkins off our plates, and sent them rollicking down the mountain.

A good thing we were so happy; and a good thing, too, that remembering my late worries over bills, I had suggested to the children not to bring more than one friend each these holidays—for so, being a manageable little party, we saw more of each other than we would have if the friends had numbered ten. A good thing this was, and that we should be so care-free and irresponsible, enjoying every minute of every day; for it was the Easter of 1914, the last Easter of the old, easy world, and our last, as well as our first, Easter as children together in the little house I had built for happiness.

§

I say as children together, because, looking back, I perceive that I too, till then, had always been one of them.

It is a painful confession to make, for no one thinks more poorly of infantilism than myself, but it did in fact need the Great War, and a second husband, to make me really grow up. The Great War was still four months off that Easter, and the second husband, biding his time in silence, was yet further, when the children and I rollicked through those last holidays seeing fun in everything, I just as immoderately amused as they were at things like my napkin being snatched out of my hand by the wind, and sent whisking down the mountain. The least thing made us laugh—oh, more than laugh, positively clap our wings and crow. Whole-heartedly we flung ourselves into any fun that offered. Life was as clear and bright as clean water. It was a picnic, an irresponsibility—just a table-napkin being tossed down the path and jubilantly chased by Coco and me, while

[*133*]

the children on the terrace, the other children, encouraged us with frantic cheers.

Absurd, happy holidays, given over to unreasonable glee, and a delicious silliness. The glee seemed to echo on in the house after I was alone again, as though there had been established in it, and for always, a habit of light-hearted happiness. At least, so I thought, and I could see no reason, as long as I kept clear of husbands, why it shouldn't be so.

Confidently, then, I tucked up my sleeves and got to work, looking forward to the next holidays, the long, summer ones, and every day walking out with Coco into an increasing glory of light and colour. All through May, all through June, the world I walked in grew more glorious. It was my first experience of mountain meadows in flower, and I rejoiced, as I walked among them, that I had pitched our tent just there. A perfect home, I said to myself, often stopping to gaze back at the blue-shuttered house tucked so snugly into the hillside, with a fringe of irises I had put in, along the edge of the terrace, just beginning to come out; I couldn't, I thought, lovingly looking at it, possibly have chosen a better one for the children and me. In it we would spend happy years together, till they married. From it the little girls would issue forth in due season, one after the other, as four little brides. And then would come the placid years in which I would practise being a grandmother, and have small children staying with me instead of big ones; and always in each year there would be a May; and always to keep me company there would be dogs and books; and always the books should be such as best egged one on *im Wahren, Guten, Schönen, resolut zu leben;* and for a long, long time the dogs would be Coco.

Fond thoughts of the care-free. They began to fade at the end of June. Like a mist over radiance, doubts drew across them, then uneasiness, and presently downright fear; and when, a month later, instead of letting the children come out to me for the summer, I went, full of forebodings and heavy of heart, to England to them, Coco was the last member of the household that I saw.

He had carried my bag in his mouth, carefully by its strap, across the fields to the point where the fly was waiting in the road to drive me down to the valley. He knew quite well I was intending to leave him, and thinking that perhaps I wouldn't do so dreadful a thing if I hadn't got my bag, he tried, when the moment came, to hold on to it. But he didn't try very hard. He was much too well-bred and polite really to put obstacles in the way of anyone's wishes. Soon he gently let me take it from him, and stood looking up at me without moving, his eyes, his sad ears, and his drooping tail saying what he had to say.

[*135*]

So I left him there, standing motionless by the side of the empty road, watching me drive away into what were to be years of deep sorrow, of acute misery—my beautiful dog, my close friend, my adoring protector, my dog I had so much loved and cared for, and who had so much loved and cared for me. And when next I saw him, five years later, he was dying.

§

Death of Coco

That was a strange thing, the death of Coco. Not that he should die, for owing to the unexpected folly of the *concierge* it was inevitable that he should, but his manner of doing it. Even at this distance of time, the remembrance agonises me.

There was a snowstorm the day of my return, alone, to the house I had left that brilliant summer afternoon five years before. A railway had meanwhile been made up the mountain, and when I got out at the little station only the *concierge* was there to meet me—no Coco.

For an instant I supposed it was because of the snowstorm, but immediately remembered that from his birth he was accustomed to every sort of mountain weather, and I asked quickly, having grown during these years very quick to be afraid, "Coco? Where is he?"

"*Il est un peu souffrant,*" said the *concierge.*

"*Souffrant? Vous avez fait venir le vétérinaire?*"

"*Pas encore. Sachant que Madame devait arriver, j'ai attendu sa permission.*"

Attendu! Oh fool, oh fool, I thought, scrambling off homewards, fighting my way through the storm, blinded by the snow, my feet slipping, my heart thumping with fear.

"But you said nothing of this in your last letter," I paused once to call back to the battling, bent figure behind.

"Three days ago he was well," came the answer, faint against the wind.

"Where is he?"

"In his kennel. He cannot move from it."

I struggled on, stumbling and slipping. Oh fool, oh fool, not at once to send for the vet, not to do everything, everything for my dog——

The last bit to the house is up a slope, very slippery in the snow—twice I fell, sprawling,—then there are steps on to the terrace, then a porch, and inside the porch the front door.

Panting I climbed that last bit, and from afar began, as well as I could, having but little breath, to whistle and call.

"Coco! Coco!" I called. "Darling dog—I've come back——"

But what was that I saw inside the porch as I got nearer, what was that dark thing stretched right across the threshold of the door, blocking it up so that I wouldn't be able to go in without stepping over it, so that whatever happened I was bound not to miss it?

Coco. Somehow struggled round from his kennel in the yard. He knew I was coming home, knew I was being fetched from the station, and with his last breath made his last effort to be with me again, for a moment, for the last moment of all.

"Coco?" I whispered, standing still, hardly able to believe it. "Oh—*Coco?*"

"It is impossible to imagine," a voice behind seemed to be saying from a great distance away, "how the dog could have reached this spot. For three days he has been immovable in his kennel."

I dropped on my knees, and took his paw in my hand. He gave the faintest wag of his tail, and tried to raise his head; but it fell back again, and he could only look at me.

For an instant, for the briefest instant, we looked at each other, and while we looked his eyes glazed.

"Coco—I've come back. Darling—I'll never leave you any more——"

I don't know why I said these things. I knew he was dead, and that no calls, no lamentations, no love could ever reach him again.

Sliding down on to the stone flags beside him, I laid my head on his and wept in an agony of bitter grief. Now indeed I was left alone in the world. Even my dog was gone.

PART III

§

DOG X

Pincher

BUT IT IS no use dwelling on agonies. There were many of them for me between my first good-bye to Coco, on the summer afternoon just before the war, and my good-bye to him for ever, in the snowstorm five years later; and all I will remark is that I hadn't known wretchedness could be packed so tight. But, as there was no dog in those years, it isn't necessary to say anything about them, which is a comfort. Who wants to write, or think, of ancient griefs? Put them on one side; cover them up with silence; take out what lessons you can from them; and then turn your back, and set your face towards any happiness that may still be left.

Such was the advice I tried to give myself as I stumbled and stammered through the next bit of my life. But griefs stick. They can't be got rid of as easily as burrs on an afternoon walk, when one pauses a moment to pick them off, and then on again. Only years, and more and more years, can wear them away at last; and suppose one hadn't got as many years as all that left?

It seemed, however, that I had. I didn't want any more, so I got them. And now I am glad, for if, as I had sometimes wished at that time, I could have finished with a consciousness become unbearable, if, in other words, I had then died, I would never have known a great many very beautiful and delightful things. Evidently, then, it is wise not too soon to lose patience with life, but to wait and see what it may have round its next corner.

I had to wait a good while. For instance, it wasn't till more than four years after Coco's death that Pincher appeared—so true is it that if you love a dog very much, and lose him, you cannot bear the thought of having another. Yet the only real cure for one's distress *is* another —I am told this also applies to lovers,—and the sooner you get him the better.

But I, obstinately mourning, spent the best part of five years without the simple comfort of a dog. What waste of time. Please God it shall never happen again. And I daresay the idiotic abstinence would have lasted even longer if an observant friend, opining that I badly needed something, and knowing it couldn't be a husband, since, from my second, I had fled, decided it must be a dog, and packed up Pincher, and sent him off.

I was living in a tiny cottage in the New Forest—sulking, it now seems to me, though then I called it by a grander name,—and hardly anybody ever came along my lane; so that when I saw the carrier's cart drawing up at my garden gate I was sure he had made a mistake, and that the box he presently brought up the path couldn't be for me.

"Live dog," he said, putting it down carefully.

Live dog? No live dog was expected, and I told him he had come to the wrong address.

"You're 'er, ain't you?" he said, turning up the label for me to look.

"Yes, I am she," I answered, being all for grammar when it happens to be the bits I know.

"Then I should let 'im out and give 'im a drink," said the carrier, preparing to depart. "Name of Pincher," he added, coming back to point to a corner of the label; and, climbing into his cart, was gone.

Pincher, hearing this conversation, had begun making a great to-do in his box, for he was thirsty, and knew the word drink as well as anybody. Whoever had sent him, and for whatever reason he was there, obviously he must be let out and given water; so I called the woman who did for me, and we opened the box and let him out,

—or rather he squeezed himself out before half the lid was off; and there is no getting away from it, I am made for dogs and dogs for me, because the instant I saw him I began to cheer up.

Sitting on the floor, I watched with admiration as he rushed round the room sniffing at everything, and making friends even with the chairs. On them he leaped, to leap off again the next minute and investigate the sofa. To finish up with he leaped on to me, sniffing my hair and my clothes, and wriggling all over with excitement.

"Oh, but aren't you a dear, funny little thing," I laughed, trying to hug his woolly body—he was a very woolly dog,—but not succeeding, because he was off round the room again.

It was a characteristic of Pincher, till that was done to him which I shall presently relate, always to be off. Never was a dog more full of eager life and insatiable curiosity. He couldn't keep still; and even when night came, and like the rest of us he had to go to bed, I believe one eye stayed awake just so as not to miss anything, just so as to be instantly ready for anything that might happen to come along.

Like that first violet of which I have written, he was the harbinger of better things, and I began to improve in mind and body from the moment of his arrival. There were his meals to see to, and his exercise; and everything I did for him seemed to do me good as well. Quite soon after he came, whenever I had a relapse into unhappiness and wanted to mop and mow some more, I went and brushed him instead, and if a fresh fit of counting up my sorrows seized me, all I had to do to cut it short was to go and count up Pincher. True he didn't outweigh the sorrows, my time for complete serenity not yet having arrived, but he certainly tipped up the balance a little, for he was a dog of the most tonic quality, the most bracing effect, and he did encourage me back to something almost like contentment. Positively, after we had been scouring the New Forest together for a few weeks, I had the feeling that my coat, too, would soon be going glossy.

§

But he chased chickens. Lamenting, I made the discovery the first time we met one. Like Ingraban (Dog III) who couldn't leave deer alone, like Prince (Dog VIII) who slew sheep, if Pincher saw a chicken he became transformed into the very spirit of murder. In the long run, this finished him. I say in the long run, because the results were not immediate, as in the case of his predecessors. Nemesis didn't come upon him hot-footed. It stalked him slowly, and got him in the end entirely owing to my own ignorance and gullibility. For where I know little, I am apt readily to believe, and one of the things I knew least about was castration.

Vaguely I was aware that it was credited with quietening, and that those who, before it, were uncontrollable, after it were uninterested. That, though, was all. I knew nothing of its ins and outs. And it wasn't till Pincher had pursued and killed my neighbour's best-laying hen— just this hen turned out to have been worth two guineas, which accordingly I paid,—that it seemed important he should be uninterested.

But how uninterest him? His excitement over hens, or anything else that moved and had a smell attached to it, was passionate, and short of being on a lead nothing would ever keep him, I was sure, from chasing such creatures. Being on a lead, though, is poor exercise for a dog. It is also poor exercise for the person at the other end of the lead. Too slow for the dog, it is too quick for the person, and, having faced the fact that on a lead he must go or run grave risks of sharing the awful fate of Prince, I now began to have the poorest time imaginable, being dragged, helter skelter, through bushes and bogs and bracken, by a strong little dog in hot pursuit of smells only he knew about.

Exhausting walks, those were. Exhausting, that is, for me, who arrived home in the utmost disorder, while

Pincher, of course, was as fresh as ever. But, like everything else, they came to an end, for one day, when a gamekeeper who had often observed us, and knew, as everybody else knew, that I had had to pay two guineas for a slaughtered hen, met us struggling together in the depths of the forest, he stopped and remarked, grinning, that my dog seemed to be a bit of a handful.

This was the beginning, though I didn't know it, of the end of that particular kind of walk, and also it was the beginning of the end of Pincher. Even if his end didn't overtake him till three years later, its first shadow fell across him then.

"Oh, he'll settle down," I panted, concerned for his reputation.

"Not he. Not unless you have him seen to," said the keeper.

"Seen to?"

"I know that sort. Nothing cures them."

"But——"

"A friend of mine'll do it for you in two twos."

"Do what?"

"See to him."

I gazed at the keeper, who was bending down patting Pincher and telling him he was a fine little chap. At the back of his mind he was no doubt thinking of his young pheasants, and their possible fate with such a dog about

—at least, that is what I surmise now, though it didn't then occur to me.

"Only wants seeing to," he said, patting. "Settle down and be quite the little gentleman after that, wouldn't you, old man. Why," he went on, straightening himself, "you'll be paying for every blessed hen in the place before you've finished, if you don't."

"Don't what?"

"See to him."

Puzzled, I asked him to explain. He did. Done every day, he said. Dog wouldn't even know. Come home smiling. He had a friend, a first-class vet——

In the end, after a second chicken had been slain, own sister it appeared to the slaughtered hen, for it cost me another two guineas, with Prince's end vivid in my memory I went to the vet, and asked him what he thought.

He thought the same as the keeper. A pleasant, reassuring man, hygienically clothed in white, he too assured me the little operation was nothing, and that if I didn't have it done there would be no peace. Quarrels with neighbours, bills for chickens, and the ultimate disappearance of the dog none would know whither, was the prospect he held out.

I gave in—that prophecy of an ultimate disappearance finally frightening me into agreement. And it was true that Pincher came home smiling. There was no apparent difference in him at all. Just the same dear little dog, sniffing my hair and trying to lick my face, with just the same, perhaps even more, eagerness for his dinner. True he didn't jump up now, or hardly at all, but nobody particularly wants dogs to jump up; and immensely relieved, immensely pleased, I warmly thanked the keeper when next I saw him, and with real enthusiasm paid the vet's bill.

But what was this I saw, presently happening to my Pincher? Wasn't he thickening rather, and doing it rather fast? Wasn't he, even while I watched him, growing curiously broader? He was indeed, and soon I could hardly lift him, and soon, instead of jumping up on chairs in the nimble way he used to, he lay supine, ever fatter and more sluggish, on the floor.

"It's because he eats so much," I said to myself, unwilling to face another possible explanation; and certainly his interest in meals, which before had been normal, and ready to break off at once if a cat or a rabbit were anywhere about, now engrossed him altogether, and the eagerness which used to be only for manly pursuits, such as the chase, was becoming daily more undividedly concentrated on food.

"Fine little chap," the hearty keeper would congratulate me, seeing me walking at my own pace in the forest, my hand, which used so painfully to clutch the straining lead, free to swing a stick or pick a flower, and a fat Pincher, very sober and giving no trouble at all, at my heels. "What did I say? Ain't he a thorough gentleman now?"

Alas, he was more than a thorough gentleman, he was a thorough lady. Worse, he was a thorough elderly lady. Worse still, he was a thorough elderly greedy lady, one for whom, all passion spent, only the pleasures of the table now remained.

Gradually these facts dawned on me, and a time came when I couldn't bear to meet the keeper, and stayed away from the forest, and couldn't bear the sight of the vet, and stayed away from the village, let alone hardly liking to look Pincher in the face, so deeply was I ashamed of what I had allowed to be done to him.

Our walks, accordingly, these other places being ruled out, became strolls in the nearest fields, and at last, as he grew fatter and slower, mere waddles in the little garden, his one idea, plainly to be read in the eyes he fixed inquiringly on me as he waddled, being to get back into the house as soon as possible, and find out what there was for dinner.

A melancholy state of things; very troubling to the conscience of the person who had brought it about. After a few weeks of this sad exercise, in a garden growing every day more damp, for autumn was upon us, it occurred to me that if waddling were to be our future we might just as well go and waddle in London. There at least I could see a few friends, and forget, while I was with them, what I had had done to Pincher. Besides, wasn't it foolish to live in the New Forest if one weren't able to go out into it? And of what earthly use were beautiful surroundings that one never saw? Further, though it was no doubt true that dogs were best in the country, this could be applied only to dogs in possession of all their faculties, and now that Pincher, through my fault, was no longer in possession of all his, he appeared to have become the very dog for London.

Thus I reasoned; and the result was that he and I, in due course, went to London, and settled in a flat; for flats, I felt, were the places obviously most suitable for the display of Pincher's negative virtues. That not wanting to move, and not wanting to make a noise, would commend him to the people next door. Housemaids would get fond of him, when they found how little trouble he gave. Liftmen wouldn't mind taking so quiet a creature up and down; and I could picture hall porters quite enjoying opening the door for one who proceeded through it with such unchanging sobriety.

So there we were, by November of that year, walking together in the mornings along the Embankment under the eye of Big Ben, and in the afternoons beneath the leafless trees of St. James's Park. Anxious to make what amends I could, I never let anyone do anything for him or take him out except myself, and he grew extremely devoted to me, poor Pincher, and if I was out at a party would sit immovable, however long it went on, just inside the door of the flat, waiting for me to come in.

Touching little dog. But being touched doesn't make one love. I am sorry to say I had left off loving Pincher. He had too many just claims on my affection, and affection won't be bounced. Nor it is easy for the wronger to love the wronged. And who, again, can be fond of a reproach that is ever present and never uttered? Poor Pincher couldn't have uttered, even if he had wanted to, but he didn't want to. Written all over him was a gross contentment. He was stupefied with contentment and food. And his being so much pleased with everything afflicted me more than any amount of bad temper, for did I not, if he had only known it, deserve the worst that he could do to me?

No, I didn't love Pincher. Apart from his wrongs and claims, he had become—my fault too,—a most dull dog, and a very odd, unattractive one to look at. But if I couldn't love him I could pretend I did, and he was no longer quick enough to notice it was only pretending. I patted and stroked him a great deal, and often, to please him, would take my hat off again when I had been going out, and stay at home with him instead,—just so that he should know I was there, and feel he might stretch out and snore comfortably by the fire, and not have to go, urged by his devotion, into the cold hall and wait for me in a draught.

"Poor old Pincher—poor, poor little dog," I would whisper softly to him, full of remorse and pity, sitting on the floor beside him and taking his head in my lap; and it made things no better that he hadn't an idea I had ever been anything but an angel to him.

§

The friend whose present he was, puzzled by his torpor and increasing bulk—I was dumb as a fish about what had happened,—began once more carefully to observe, and, having observed, opined that there was something wrong with the dog.

Such bulk, the friend explained, while I sat uneasily by, was unnatural, and must be due to the torpor, and the torpor was due to his being, so to speak, an only child. Give him a playmate, said the friend, and I would soon see a difference.

Too well did I know I wouldn't; but, not wishing to

[*155*]

embark on explanations, I merely threw cold water on the playmate. More than one dog in a London flat would be impossible, I said; and anyhow the management wouldn't allow it.

"Try," said the friend, looking thoughtfully at Pincher's broad body and small, almost disappearing head; adding that, though he wasn't much more than a year old, he might easily, from his appearance and behaviour, be taken for ten.

Such remarks made me feel very bad. Only too well did I know that Pincher's age, through my fault, was indeed the equivalent of ten. And a poor ten, too; ten, already nearly senile. Still, there it was, and no playmate would ever change it; so I stood out obstinately against the suggestion, even going so far as to declare that all it would do to the dog would be to plunge him into acute fits of jealousy.

Acute fits! The contented, passive little lump on the rug didn't look much like acute fits of anything. He was past that. He was definitely *jenseits des Guten und Bösen*. But I wasn't going to say so and provoke questions difficult to answer, and stooping down to pat my poor dog very gently, very apologetically, I murmured that we were perfectly content, he and I, to have only each other.

There is no stopping friends, however, when once they

are bent on doing what they imagine will be a kindness, and the playmate arrived next day. Without either further argument or by your leaves, it was sent round in a basket.

I thought the basket had violets in it. It was March, and everywhere in London were violets. The shops were full of them; the street corners were massed with them; and I called my maid to bring a bowl and water, while I cut the string and opened the lid.

But this wasn't violets. Curled up snugly, its head between its paws, and looking at me with great gravity out of the corner of one lifted eye, was a little smooth white creature, with a card tied round its neck on which was written: *I am Knobbie. A young lady three months old. Try me on Pincher.*

§

DOG XI

Knobbie

WE LOOKED at each other. She lay motionless, merely keeping that lifted eye on me. Pincher, indifferent before

[*157*]

the fire, didn't even trouble to raise his head, nor did she take any notice of him, though she must have smelt him because, since I had had him seen to, even if one weren't a dog one easily smelt poor Pincher.

In his direction, however, she didn't so much as twitch a nostril. It was on me that her attention was concentrated, and I wouldn't have supposed a single eye could hold so much in it of grave appraisement. What she saw I cannot say, for who shall guess how we appear to dogs? But what I saw was a baby fox-terrier, snow white except for her ears, which were—and are; she is sitting beside me as I write,—a lovely glossy chestnut, divided from each other by a straight, broad band of more white.

Perfect and spotless, as though that very morning she had had her bath and breakfast in Paradise, she lay completely unembarrassed, waiting for what I would do next, and merely looked at me with that lifted eye. "Knobbie," I said, almost with a bow, as though introducing her to myself; and almost it seemed as if she bowed back, as if she made a small, polite movement of her head. I have known dogs do more surprising things than that. Winkie, for instance, once, when he was going to be sick—

But I haven't got to Winkie yet.

"Would you like me to lift you out of your basket, Knobbie?" I asked, very politely, for she somehow brought out politeness in others.

Apparently she had no objection, and taking her in my two hands—she was like satin to touch, and as smooth as plumpness could make her,—I put her carefully down on the floor, and was enchanted to find that the first thing she did was not to wet the carpet.

This was a great thing. Ingo and Ivo (Dogs VI and VII) the only other puppies I had ever had—except Bijou, who doesn't count,—did nothing but wet carpets, though they were six months old when they first came, against Knobbie's three. But she was a lady. I now know that ladies, in the dog world, wouldn't dream of doing such a thing, once it has been pointed out to them as undesirable. They are most elegantly clean and particular, and will wait almost any time to be put out of doors, rather than behave as they shouldn't. Of this, though, I was then unaware, and not wishing to take any risks, besides being anxious that so bright a beginning should remain undimmed, I took her up in my arms, and a second time was enchanted, for she snuggled.

There was no doubt about it: she did snuggle, and she was the first of my dogs to do so. Great Danes, in the nature of things, can't snuggle, and all the others—except Bijou, who doesn't count,—had been grown up. Of course I was enchanted. Of course my heart glowed, as the little thing pressed against me and tucked her head confidently beneath my chin. All good women, and most good men, go on having maternal instincts to the very end, and adore it when something small and helpless is so obliging as to show its trust by snuggling—especially, I think, women in my then situation, whose husbands, for one cause or another, aren't there, and whose children are married and living in far away countries. Such women, however haughtily they may say, "*I* don't want anybody to love me," do in fact often want, in a vague, uneasy sort of way, everybody to love them, and should this wish narrow down, as it occasionally does, from everybody to somebody, there may be trouble.

It is then that dogs come in. It was then that Knobbie came in. Not that I would suggest I myself had been in the condition just described, but the truth is that life, as it proceeds, does become a good deal pruned of its simpler joys, which are mostly connected with the love and rearing of one's young. These certainly had now been pruned from me. My days of rearing children were done. My love could follow them only in spirit. So that there was an outward bareness, a seeming emptiness about my life at that time, which was apparently noticeable, since my friend had observed it and had tried to clothe and fill it with Pincher.

Here he had failed, for reasons, he was never told; but, trying again with Knobbie, he succeeded, for if Pincher's

arrival had set me off recovering some of the balance I
had lost, Knobbie's arrival completed my cure.

An odd effect for a single small puppy to produce;
but not more odd than the effect a single lilac-bush,
flowering in the sun one May morning, produced on a
woman I know. She had meant, being more full of griefs
than she felt she could conveniently hold, to finish with
life that day, but, taking a turn in the garden first, she
saw this bush, and having seen it thought that perhaps
she had better wait a little. For, she argued, a world that
can produce such beauty shouldn't lightly be left; and I
too, holding the snuggly little warm Knobbie in my arms,
perceived again, after a space of years, that the world
had many most admirable sides, and that the best thing
I could do was once more to seek and ensue them.

And there sighed through my mind the word *resolut,*
as if the old vow were turning in its sleep.

Im Wahren, Guten, Schönen resolut zu leben . . .

Why, not, I asked myself, my cheek on Knobbie's soft
ears, have another try?

§

But it is no use having tries at things like that in London. At least, it was no use for me. I found I couldn't

be *resolut* in company. At a party, I simply forgot the *Wahr* and *Gut* and *Schön*. Such gatherings had much the same effect on me as telephones—they deflected me from that which I like to believe is my true self. With concern and shame, I noted that my ear at them was basely cocked for flattery, and all my thoughts were finicking. No wonder when, after one of them, I at last got home to the simple Pincher, waiting up for me so patiently on the doormat, and the guileless Knobbie sweetly sleeping in her basket, and at sight of these two innocents regained some, at least, of my scattered self-possession, no wonder I would then ask myself whether parties were really worth while.

They weren't. They never have been, for me. Friends, too, though delightful, seemed, at those moments of weariness, only delightful if properly spaced, and how is one to space anybody or anything in London? Of everything there, there appeared to be too much. And I would sit despondent on the edge of the bed, and fall to remembering the roomy years in Pomerania, when only every six months did we go to, or give, a party, and the glorious times I had had in Switzerland between the visits of guests, when Coco and I were alone with mountains.

From these meditations it did finally appear that I wasn't suited to crowds, and Knobbie, judging by her behaviour when I took her out for exercise in the Park, was evidently not suited to them either. The noise of the traffic, as I carried her across Whitehall, terrified her. That composure which so charmed me when we were in the flat, disappeared entirely out of doors, and the mere sight of another dog approaching in the distance was enough to make her almost faint. Plainly, conventual life was best for my thin-skinned, inexperienced young lady, and it appeared best for me too, if I seriously meant to do anything about being *resolut*. There remained Pincher to be considered, but Pincher was content wherever he was as long as it included me and dinner, so one fine day, with him waddling at my heels, and Knobbie tucked under my arm, I turned my back on London, and went again to live in the country.

Very different were my feelings now from the ones I had had when I fled into the New Forest, to hide and forget. It wasn't only, I believe, that time had been at its usual work of healing, of glossing over—it was also that I was accompanied by dogs. There had been no dog with me during the lamentable years which included Coco's death and ended with the arrival of Pincher; if there had been, I might sooner have got mended. Now, with two of them, even if one was more a burden than a joy, I went off confidently, sure it was the best thing for a person who was still, I suppose, what my Aunts

Charl and Jessie called peculiar, while as for Knobbie, I felt it would save her reason.

Really I was very much obliged to Knobbie, whose nerves gave me the necessary push-off. Without her, I might have lingered on in London indefinitely, and became permanently convivial.

§

Pincher took me to London, and Knobbie brought me away. It looked as if I were beginning to be led about by dogs.

My relations, indeed, pointed this out, and expressed regret. They used the word infatuation, and said infatuation was always a pity. But I paid no heed, for he who heeds relations won't get anywhere, not even into the country, and on getting into the country I was absolutely bent.

This time, though, I didn't go farther than twenty miles out, so that I would still be able easily to visit friends for a few hours, should I have a relapse into gregariousness; yet, although so near London, the effect of being in pure country was complete, because the house, standing alone, faced golf links, and on its other three sides was surrounded by woods.

[*164*]

In these woods were endless safe paths for Knobbie, where she would never meet a soul, while for Pincher there was a roomy garden in which he could lie and pant comfortably, with ancient trees to shade him should he be inconvenienced by the sun. The day we took possession there was no sun, but since sun, sooner or later, is bound to shine, its absence didn't at the moment disturb me, and we settled in in high good humour—at least, Knobbie and I did, and I think Pincher too must have been in some sort of good spirits beneath his outer apathy, for the first thing he got was an extra big dinner.

I thought it a very charming little house. It breathed peace and silence. The woods, dressed for autumn, brooded close over it at the back, and in front stretched the golf-course, empty that day because of fog. Outside the sitting-room window was a dovecote, filled, by the same friend who had given me my dogs, with doves whose cooings were to soothe me while I worked; and on the hearth-rug, also a present from this same—ought I not now to call him zoological?—friend, sat a coal-black cat for luck, which at once took to Knobbie, and began diligently tidying and washing her ears.

Tea was brought; curtains were drawn; the firelight danced; the urn hissed. We might have been a picture in a romance, when the pen, swerving a moment aside from high life, pauses on a simple cottage interior. And while I ate muffins—things I had never been able even to look at in London, but now swallowed with complacence,—and Pincher sat in front of me watching every mouthful, just as though he hadn't had an enormous dinner a few minutes before, and the cat, finished with Knobbie's ears, deftly turned her over and began tidying her stomach, I did feel that my feet were set once more in the path of peace, and that all I had to do was to continue steadily along it.

§

So did I enter upon a fresh lap of that solitude decorated with dogs which, each time it had been my portion, had given me such contentment.

It was Knobbie, of course, who decorated, growing every day more charming now that she was freed from fear, for Pincher, since I had had him seen to, couldn't any longer be called an ornament. Yet he had been a personable little dog when first he came. That he should have become odd-looking enough for no small boy to be able to pass him in silence was entirely my fault, and I regarded the comments he roused during his daily exercise on the Embankment, while I lived in London, as part of my just punishment.

I was glad to get away from these comments into the quiet country, for they used to force me to walk with my head unnaturally high, pretending I heard nothing or, if I heard, that I didn't care—especially during those trying moments, familiar to all who take their dogs on leads, when I had to stand still and wait.

What could I do, faced by derision, except hold my head high and pretend to be deaf? I found it very difficult, though, because often what I heard made me want to laugh. "See that there dawg?" a tram-conductor called one day to anybody who would listen, his tram having happened to pause just where I, too, was being obliged to pause by Pincher, "I know 'is pedigree, I do. 'Is mother was a 'edge 'og, and 'is father a blinking fool."

Always I was thankful when it was time to go back to the cover of the flat; but now, in the spacious garden round the cottage, everything was easy, and my poor hedgehog—he really did look rather like one,—could be turned loose, and needn't be taken for walks. It was a great relief, I think, to him, and certainly it was a relief to me who, apart from not enjoying rousing the mirth of passers-by, would any day rather run with Knobbie than waddle with Pincher. But unfortunately, just as he used to wait on the doormat of the flat until I came home, so did he wait at the gate, however cold or wet it might be, for me to reappear, and I was always being dragged back from my walks long before Knobbie, who had developed the swiftness and grace of a greyhound, had had enough, by the vision of that patient little image sitting there stolidly, and determined not to budge till he got me again.

And when he had got me again, what did he do? He went to sleep. It was all he wanted—to go to sleep, knowing I was there. Indeed, that was all Pincher ever wanted, besides his dinner: that I should stay by his side, while he snored. Which annoyed me, for after all he wasn't a husband.

§

Here is Knobbie the following summer, grown by that time into a great girl, and turning her head away from Pincher.

He isn't in the picture, because just as I was taking it he waddled away, caring as little for Knobbie's company as she for his. From first to last she turned her head away from him, while he, for his part, didn't give a rap for her. But then, of course, the poor dog hadn't any raps, whatever they may be, to give, and if it hadn't been for the cat, Knobbie might have spent a lonely, play-starved childhood. The cat, however, did what it could, and they had a good deal of fun together till Chunkie,

yet another present from the same friend, joined our party; whereupon Knobbie, staring at the unexpected apparition of a brand-new puppy marching so confidently into the room, as though it were his room and she and the cat and Pincher belonged to him too, for ever forgot such things as cats, and fell head over ears in love.

It was a *coup de foudre*. I had heard of *coups de foudre*, but never either experienced one or witnessed one being administered. With my own eyes I now beheld *foudre* hurtling down on Knobbie. Chunkie, a semi-Sealyham puppy ten weeks old, incredibly small and cocky and game, had only to swagger in, look insolently round, give a loud bark or two which said as plainly as words that he was ready to take on the lot of us, for her instantly to become his slave.

§

DOG XII

Chunkie

CHUNKIE was, and is, a charmer of the first order. He is curled up in my lap as I write, and the paper is propped on his sleeping back.

Here is his picture when he was four months old, the funny markings on his face, like raised eyebrows, to which everyone at once succumbed, giving him an air of permanent astonishment.

But I wish I had been able to take a photograph of him the day the door of the sitting-room opened, and he appeared, alone and unannounced. The chauffeur who

brought him, discreetly didn't show himself, leaving him to make his own impression, and never could I have believed anything so small could be so fearless, or anything, plunged into the middle of complete strangers, all much bigger than himself, be so cocky.

His tail, proud symbol of an unconquerable spirit, stuck up gaily, and has stuck up ever since. Not once have I seen it lowered during the whole five years I have had him, not even when, outraged by his behaviour, which is often reprehensible—he is a great lover, and will run miles and stay away hours, risking being stolen, run over or shot, if there is any lovemaking to be done, —when, I say, outraged by such behaviour I raise an indignant hand against him, his tail, instead of drooping, wags, and his eyes, fixed on my face, are the eyes of one who knows he has done wrong, but thinks it was well worth it. At once smug, ingratiating and defiant, he looks me boldly in the face, and my hand falls nerveless at my side. After all, I can't help being glad he has enjoyed himself, and anyhow I am deeply thankful to have got him safe home again.

That friend who is now becoming monotonous as a giver, in giving me Chunkie added him to what my relations were beginning to speak of as a menagerie, and he added him because, when the second winter at the cottage loomed close, he thought he saw signs of restiveness in me, of a tendency to walk to the window and scowl at the weather, of a desire that seemed to him excessive, to whom such things meant nothing, for more sunshine than England provided; and having observed these signs for a time in silence, opined that what I needed was another dog. To steady me. To hold me down in the place I was in already. For if, he reckoned, a woman could easily go abroad with one dog, and not so easily with two, with three it would be so difficult that she wouldn't attempt it, and, loving all three, she would be quite unable to leave them, would stay where she was, and her friends could continue to come down and have tea with her.

Such were his simple calculations, which up to a point were correct. Where they went wrong was in taking for granted, after Chunkie's arrival, that I loved three dogs. I didn't; I only loved two. In regard to Pincher, all I felt was self-reproachful responsibility, and at any time since I had had him seen to would gladly have parted from him, if I could have found him a good home. But naturally I never told my friend this, whose gift he was, and for all his observing he hadn't noticed that Pincher wasn't in my heart.

For all his observing, too, he didn't find out the reason why I dreaded another winter in the cottage. Ours was a friendship based on, and chiefly nourished by, dogs; that is how I, at least, saw it, keeping myself otherwise a good deal to myself. Opine as he might, he at no time really *knew,* and the last things I would ever have talked to him about would have been my secret disappointments and shames.

There he would sit, the days he came to call, quietly having tea surrounded by his four-legged gifts, and he hadn't an idea that a few hours before, during the heavy, hopeless rain of the morning, I had been gnawing my knuckles because of my inability, increasing with each wet day, to be *resolut* in bad weather.

No doubt one has often sat thus at tea among people sleek with muffins, imperturbable of aspect, and in con-

[*173*]

versation calm, who weren't at all like that inside—
people who, perhaps, too that very morning had been
gnawing their knuckles over some secret trouble. How
can one tell from outsides? For all I knew my zoological
friend might be actually gnawing his in spirit at that very
minute, while he sat so apparently placid by the fire; but
I don't think so, because he was a man of one idea, which
was to give me dogs, and to have one idea only does tend
to promote that inner tidiness which is peace.

But I, after ten weeks of almost constant cold down-
pours, was making the shameful discovery that those
plans for living resolutely, which had brought me away
from London and lodged me in a noble solitude, came to
nothing if it rained. In other words, though I wanted as
much as ever to seek and ensue the *Wahr* and *Gut* and
Schön, I could only do so, with any real zest, if the sun
shone.

No wonder I gnawed my knuckles. The disconcerting
discovery took all the wind out of my sails. I was ashamed
to death. But there it was, and being ashamed didn't stop
the cold rain, and the cold rain gave me chilblains, and
chilblains upset everything. Especially upsetting was it to
remember that I hadn't been and felt like this in my
mountain home, where the wind roared, and the rain
dashed against the windows for weeks on end, without
quenching a single spark of my inner glow. Probably I

[*174*]

had had chilblains there too, but they had so little affected my spirit that I couldn't even be sure. Was it that I was older now? Was this perhaps the way, the trivial, contemptible way, age was going to manifest itself —in ups and downs, in dependence on warmth, and in an extreme distaste for clouds that didn't go away?

Age. I had never till then thought about it, except for other people. Now, for the first time, the idea that I too perhaps might soon get old, was, perhaps, already beginning to, entered my head; and I was much struck by it.

§

There was another friend of mine—a woman this time, —who was living beautifully in the sun. In Provence she lived, and on one of her visits to London she came down to see me, bringing into the room with her that dark afternoon, I thought, all the radiance of the south. The light and warmth of a more blessed climate seemed still to linger round her, she seemed still to reflect the sunshine she had left, and whenever she moved I fancied there was delicately shaken into the air a fragrance of sweet flowers, such as jasmine.

"Why not come and live near me?" she said. "I know a little house among olive-trees. In November"—it was

[*175*]

then November,—"the grass round it is thick with those long-stalked, pink and white daisies."

Strange how few words are needed to alter one's whole life. I didn't then know those long-stalked, pink and white daisies, but I know them now, and it is in that little house, expanded at each end to a greater roominess and turned the colour of honeysuckle, that I am at this moment writing—changed from a shivering creature brittle with cold, who tries, by blowing on her fingers, to be able after breakfast to hold a pen, into one who no longer has to hope it may be fine tomorrow, because it invariably is; or, if not quite invariably tomorrow, certainly the day after.

I cannot tell how other people feel, but to me this makes the entire difference between praising God for my creation, preservation, and all the blessings of my life, and remaining ominously silent. If only I had come here straight from Pomerania—concentrated, from the very beginning of that freedom to choose where to live which characterises widows, on light, heat, colour and fragrance,—how good it would have been for my disposition! Instead of becoming mellow merely by dint of growing older, I would have mellowed young; instead of having moments of despair, I would have been unshakably serene. Impossible not to catch some, at least, of the serenity, the urbanity, of the skies under which one lives. When beauty is all round one it is bound to get into one's spirit and stay there. I walk in beauty— not like Byron's lady who walked in her own, but in the beauty of light, heat, colour and fragrance. Easy enough to be *resolut* here. It is child's play. It is one's normal condition. And if it weren't that dogs are what I am writing about, I would pause a moment to set down the many reasons I have for blessing the friend who brought me to this place.

§

Death of Pincher

Knobbie and Chunkie came with me to Provence, but Pincher, during the year we had to wait in the cottage on the golf course for the honeysuckle-house to be added to and got ready, grew so old, so heavy, so almost entirely immovable, that it seemed it would be a kindness, rather than leave him with anyone I wasn't quite sure of, to have him put to sleep.

I did all I could to find a home for him, for still he loved his dinner, and the thought that he would never have another at a word from me was distressing. But nobody I could trust wanted poor Pincher. Whoever I offered him to, invariably answered he would be pleased to take Chunkie. Even the friend who gave him to me declined to have him back, on the ground that he wasn't the dog he used to be—didn't I know it?—and that although he was now only three years old, he might well have been thirty.

"For each year in a normal dog's life," said my friend, thoughtfully observing him, "this dog seems to advance ten."

And since thirty is no age for a dog, and it wasn't to be supposed that forty would be any better, and no one wanted him, and I couldn't take him with me, everything pointed to his being put to sleep.

But it is a terrible thing actually to give the order that launches a living creature into the eternal cold of death. Here was Pincher today, warm and content, still able to lie by the fire and snore, still adoring his dinner; how could I bring myself to stop him from having a tomorrow? I couldn't. I didn't. I put it off and off, and he kept on having tomorrows, and dinners of an increasing, solicitous lavishness.

Poor little Pincher. Not till our very last day at the cottage, when it had become inevitable, did the vet, who had taken care of that which my relations now called Whipsnade, come over, and after the poor dog had had a final dinner—a banquet, really, of all the things he liked best,—put him gently and comfortably to sleep.

He was buried in the garden. I wish my end may be as easy. But even now, five years afterwards, I never can think of Pincher without remorse.

§

If this weren't a book about dogs only, I might here dwell on a great-grandfather I had, and his daughter my great-aunt, who both died like Pincher, after an extra good dinner. No vet was needed in their case; the dinner did it. Warned, my great-grandfather defied; and tradition insists that his last words were that he didn't care what anybody said, duck and green peas were worth any amount of dying. My great-aunt, of the same dogged, indomitable blood, in her turn made similar statements, it is said, though what she died of was, more ignobly I think, cod. But since I am not here writing of my ancestry but about Chunkie and Knobbie, let me get back to them, whose children were born in the honeysuckle-coloured house—a house already scrambled over, almost to its roof, by the eager roses of the south.

Chunkie, once he was grown-up, was not the dog to put off getting married, and having been frequently thwarted in this wish by my interference and by the fact that he was lower on the ground than Knobbie, became artful, watched his opportunity, found it when she was going downstairs one day in front of him, seized it, and nine weeks later the pledges of their loves were born on my bedroom sofa.

I could have wished she had chosen a different place. I never expected the *accouchement* to happen in my house, and had made all arrangements for her to go to a nursing-home well ahead, as I thought, of the time. But my calculations were a week out, and one night while I was quietly reading, and she was lying at my feet apparently asleep, she suddenly got up, turned round, sat down straight in front of me, and stared.

She stared so hard that it pierced through the covers of my book, and putting it down I asked her if she wanted to go out.

She didn't move—merely went on staring; and I, inexperienced in such occasions, began to read again. But I couldn't fix my attention. Those eyes on the other side of the book bored through it, and presently I got up and went to the door, and encouraged her to go out into the garden. Instead, she hurried up to my bedroom, jumped on the sofa, and began having puppies.

The house immediately woke to activity. My maid, who was tidying the room, dropped everything and came running down, with loud cries announcing what was going on on the sofa. I flew upstairs; bells rang; feet scuttled; the chauffeur rushed away to fetch the vet; and only Knobbie, among the lot of us, was calm.

To see the way she behaved before the vet appeared, after whose arrival she placed herself, with touching confidence, entirely in his hands, one would have imagined it to be her tenth confinement instead of her first. She knew exactly what to do with each puppy as it arrived, and did it. She was composure itself, only asking, till the vet came, to be let alone. And by the time she had done, there were six puppies—two born dead because, said the vet, of that jump on to the sofa.

Here is a picture of her three weeks later, proudly nursing the four who were left:

And here is another, in which she is looking a little worried and reproachful at that one of her children who, in fact, turned out to be the bad boy of the family. And

here, too, is one of myself being crawled over by them a little later still, when they were grown very perfect in my eyes.

I think I was as proud of them as Knobbie was. I know she couldn't have loved them more than I did.

One consequence, though, of her motherhood, and I thought it very odd, was that she took a deep dislike to Chunkie. It wasn't as if she hadn't had a perfectly easy confinement; she owed him no grudge on account of agony. Yet there she was, evidently disliking him very

much, making the most dreadful faces at him whenever he sauntered past, and if he dared so much as cock an eye in the direction of his offspring her growls were frightening.

My gentle Knobbie, transformed to savagery by precisely the experience which is supposed to soften a lady out of all knowledge! I watched her in astonishment, remembering the extreme devotion she used to show Chunkie, how she couldn't bear him out of her sight, coaxing him to play with her, flattering him by laughing with eager diligence at what I presume were his jokes— and if there are still people who say dogs don't laugh, let them look at this picture of Knobbie doing it: Is she not laughing? And has not Chunkie something of the air of the skilled *raconteur,* who has made his point and is resting gravely on his laurels, while the audience gives way to the expected mirth?

Dogs are for ever reminding me of myself. I know I must often have looked like this picture of Knobbie when, before I married them, I laughed at the good stories of those who became my husbands. Naturally I couldn't laugh quite so wholeheartedly later on, when marriage had made me familiar with the stories, but repetition does have the advantage of enabling the listener to know the exact right moment to throw back his or her head, like Knobbie, and begin to roar.

When this picture was taken, though, she was in the days of her care-free girlhood. After that, she laughed no more. From the birth of her puppies on, nothing that Chunkie could do, no joke, however amusing, that he might communicate to her in the mysterious way dogs do communicate, would get a smile out of her. Less courteous—or shall I say less abject?—and more honest than myself, she simply didn't bother to laugh. Her thoughts were only for her children. The nuzzling little creatures took up her whole attention; and they took up the whole of mine too, I found, because four puppies, once they begin to crawl about, need a great deal of looking after.

For a long while I tried to believe that I would be able to keep them all, so equally enchanting did they seem, but as they grew bigger this belief faded, it became more and more difficult to cope with so many, and at last I was obliged, with the greatest reluctance and most sorrowfully, to give two away to friends.

For all that, I still had four dogs, and my relations, getting wind of it, wrote and said it was a pity. "You are becoming," they wrote, "all dog——," and really I sometimes felt that way myself, so much absorbed had I to be, of necessity, in the four, if they were to have their just dues as regards runs, grooming, food, and, where the puppies were concerned, training in those ways of cleanliness which alone would bring them peace.

[*185*]

Four dogs not only seem, but are, a great many, and I wasn't surprised by my relations' comments. What, though, they didn't know was the excessive pleasure, amusement and exercise I got out of them. True the exercise sometimes appeared to be a little much, and when I was tired I was inclined to think that perhaps I ought to have started on this sort of thing younger; but anyhow the eighteen months during which all four were with me were much the gayest and liveliest, if also the most breathless, of my life.

I would recommend those persons who are inclined to stagnate, whose blood is beginning to thicken sluggishly in their veins, to try keeping four dogs, two of which are puppies. Not leaving them to servants; really keeping them.

§

DOGS XIII AND XIV

Woosie and Winkie

THE TWO I finally picked out to keep were Woosie and Winkie. As to Winkie, I never had a doubt that he was my dog, so evident, quite early, was his intelligence and sensitiveness. Pure white, except the right side of his face, which was black, and except for one big black spot in the middle of his left ear, he quickly stood out from the rest by his affectionateness and devotion to me. He was a one-man dog, and I, as soon as he was old enough to know his own mind, was his man.

Here he is, when he was a year old, sitting on my proud lap:

Over Woosie I hesitated, weighing him up a good while against the merits of the other two, and finally deciding on him because he seemed, of the litter, to be the only one like Chunkie.

Seemed. No reality, as it turned out, could have had a greater discrepancy with its appearance. Chunkie was a very adorable dog, and Woosie wasn't. Their coats were the same, but not their characters. Afterwards, when it was too late and I had given the other two away, I was surprised at my blindness in being taken in by such a superficial resemblance. Except for the coat, by the time Woosie was two months old there wasn't a shred of likeness to his enchanting father. His head had none of the generous width of Chunkie's, but was a narrow, oddly bumpy affair, and his eyes, which almost had a cast in them, were without a spark of the easy good-nature, the kindly live-and-let-live expression, that shone so attractively in Chunkie's. If I had been more experienced, the shape of his head and the almost crookedness of his eyes would have warned me, but on the strength of his curly coat I chose him, and the minute he was old enough to get really going, he revealed himself as a thorough-paced little devil.

Here he is, whispering obviously bad things in Winkie's innocent ear, while his father sits disapprovingly apart:

How the saintly Knobbie could have produced such a child, I can't think; how two such delightful parents could have had a son like that is a mystery. For a long while I didn't believe his snaps and growls were in earnest, but supposed they were just fun. They were, anyhow, diminutive, matching his diminutive size; but as he grew bigger so did they, and it was a shock one day to realise that if Winkie hadn't happened to be bigger still, there wouldn't have been much of him left. Even as it was, he got torn about sometimes. That white ear with the black spot in its middle, which was my special pride, was in constant danger of being rent asunder, and very soon I was obliged to interfere in what I had so long

[*189*]

supposed were games, and face the fact that Woosie was a bad little dog, whose playing was really nothing but bitter strife.

Especially upsetting was it if he started quarrelling in the car. It was my practice, when they were old enough, to drive them out with their parents every afternoon at three o'clock—before, that is, the hour at which I was liable to get caught in the wash of social merriment which convulses the *Côte d'Azur* from five in the afternoon till an hour, deep in the night, which I have never investigated. I drove them to woods and fields, far enough from main roads for them to be able to run in safety. Directly the car came round, the four of them leapt into it, three on the back seat and Knobbie in front beside me, and alarmingly often, instead of sitting all good and quiet like the others, Woosie would begin to fight.

It is highly unpleasant to drive a car in which dogs are fighting. I know of nothing more difficult and frightening. If you stop and tumble them out into the road, they risk being run over. If you stop and don't tumble them out, you are more or less certain to come out torn and bleeding yourself. But on the whole it was safer to stop, and I used to draw up by the side of the road with as little wobble as I could manage under the circumstances, and then, safe at least from collisions with other cars, leaned over and did my best, by grabs and minatory exhortations, to separate the struggling mass at the back.

Knobbie never fought, but when a fight was going on withdrew into her corner as far as she could, and looked pained. Chunkie never began a quarrel, but once it had started couldn't resist having a go at it too. Flinging himself into the fray, he fought with a thoroughness and gusto that scared me, because his little belly was very round and tightly stretched, and a stray jab from one or other of his infuriated sons' teeth might have punctured it. However, it never did get punctured, nor were any of us ever seriously wounded, though from the noise and violence one would have supposed nobody could come out of that car alive, let alone whole; and at least going home there was peace, and we arrived in some sort of order, because by that time they had had their run and were exercised into quiet.

But what a lot of exercise they needed, before they reached this state! Surely of all races the terrier race is the most lively? Every day our walks seemed to have to be longer, to keep pace with their growing strength, and it was no use trying to evade my share of the exercise by sitting down on a tree-trunk while they chased each other, for if I did they instantly left off doing whatever they had been doing, and sat down too—fidgeting, whining, quivering with impatience to be off again, but not stirring till I got up and went on.

It was extremely wearing. They had been born on All Saints' Day, which, as every choirboy knows, is November 1st, and by the time they were old enough to be tireless the warmths of April and May had begun. Not so easy, I found, for me to be violently active in a southern spring. It didn't affect them, though, and headed by the fleet and graceful Knobbie, and tailed by the short-legged but indomitable Chunkie, they would stream across the fields as though no such thing as heat existed, while I, far behind, laboured along, thankful if I didn't lose sight of the four little white bodies.

For me, the only really pleasant moment of our outings was when we got back to the car. Then, having safely shut them in, with a sigh of relief I could sink into the driving-seat and praise God that I needn't, at least for that day, walk any farther. Yet, really, great was my reward for those daily exertions. They did stretch me, and lighten me, and prevent the sorts of curves collecting which nobody cares to have, they did stave off the moment, which I suppose easily arrives for those who accumulate rather than shed, of being short of breath and extended of outline; and certainly till then I had never known the sheer deliciousness of sitting still.

"We are told," wrote my relations, "that you are growing thin. Scragginess is never becoming. It is, of course, all those dogs."

Here they are, all those dogs, waiting to be let out of

the car on getting home from one of our outings. Knob-bie is on the left, then Chunkie, then Winkie, and then Woosie.

I can't help thinking that, even in this moment of calm, Woosie looks a bad little dog, alert for opportunities of evil.

§

Death of Woosie

Nevertheless, when he died I grieved. A gifted friend who stayed with me that summer, one who broke out easily into noble verse, wrote thus of my house and its then contents:

This is the home of Graces and of Muses.
It's also Knobbie's, Chunkie's, Winkie's, Woosie's.

Alas, it didn't stay Woosie's long. Hardly was the ink dry on that couplet than it ceased to apply to the poor dog, for he was cruelly snatched away by death; and it made it no less distressing that it should have been his own fault, his own defiant disobedience, which hurried him off to his doom.

Early in his career it was apparent that Woosie had no intention of ever obeying anybody. I might whistle till breath failed, call, threaten, beseech, cajole, and he would still continue unheedingly to do whatever happened at the moment to be interesting him. If, having finally got him back by the ignominious method of fetching him, I proposed to spank him, he, for his part, at once proposed to bite, and sometimes did; if, in order to prevent further departures, I put him on a lead, he sat down and refused, unless actually dragged, to stir. I couldn't bring myself to drag him, therefore he didn't stir; and presently, defeated, I would take the lead off, pick him up, and ignoring his furious snappings and struggles carry him a while—just to show that, positively, he had to come along with the rest of us, and not go rushing off so dangerously on his own account.

But what was the good of that? The minute I put him down—and I soon had to, for nobody can carry a struggling dog very far,—off he darted again, sometimes luring Winkie who, left to himself, was exquisitely obedient, to dart off after him. Winkie, however, I easily persuaded back. At all times he was only happy if he knew I was near, and though he would stream off with the others in the first excitement of being let out of the car, he alone of the pack would stop every now and then, and look round to see if I were coming. So that he was as safe as his more experienced parents crossing roads— waiting, on arriving at one, till I reached it too, and then hurrying across it with me at the word of command.

But Woosie never dreamed of either waiting for me or,

when we crossed it, hurrying. The only occasions on which he seemed to be leisurely were in the middle of a road. There he would loiter, he who never loitered, and sniff in absorbed examination of any objects of interest, behaving as if such things as cars swooping round corners, and bearing down on him with relentless French impetuosity, didn't exist.

It was his death. A day came when the others and I had, as usual, hurried across a road which seemed quite quiet, and he, as usual, stayed loitering in the middle. Arrived on the other side, I called and whistled as usual, and as usual no notice was taken. It was only a secondary country road, on which I had never yet seen any traffic, so that I didn't at once go back and catch hold of him, as I would have if it had been a *route nationale,* but walked on a few paces through the scrub of sage and rock-roses, exhorting him, over my shoulder, to be a good dog and come along; and those few paces were enough to make it impossible to get to him in time to save him when a car came rushing round the corner.

On him before I could even begin to run, it continued its way in complete indifference to what it had left behind in the road. He was still alive, but unconscious, when I reached him, and picking him up I drove frantically to the nearest vet, with the other three dogs huddled, appalled, in the back.

On the way the poor mangled thing came to, and then began horror. I had to slow down for fear of adding to his agony, and it seemed as if we would never get to the vet's. Suppose, too, the vet should be out when we did get there? Oh, I have been thankful often in my life, deeply thankful, but never more deeply than when I found that man was in.

Together we carried my unhappy little dog to the operating table, where, quieter by then, he lay as he was put, his eyes fixed on me to whom, strong and well, he had paid so little heed. In this last dreadful moment I was his only hope—and what a hope! Somebody who could do nothing for him except stroke his poor head and whisper, desperate for the vet to be quick and end such sufferings, "You'll soon be better, darling—soon be better . . ."

He seemed, though, to understand and believe. He never took his eyes off my face till the blessed sleep the vet was giving him gradually dimmed them. He couldn't have lived. He was most grievously damaged. And what, I asked the vet when it was over, about the people in the car, who knew what they had done—for I saw them, while I was still struggling through the bushes, looking out of the back window,—and yet drove on indifferently? Did he suppose that in all the wide world there could be forgiveness for such people?

He shrugged his shoulders. *"Après tout, madame,"* he said, *"ce n'est qu'un chien."*

§

It seemed to me as I drove home, with Woosie wrapped in a cloth I had begged of the vet, at my feet—Woosie so quiet now, who had never yet been quiet, so for ever acquiescent,—it seemed to me as if I saw for the first time, in their just proportions, the cruelty and suffering which is life, and the sure release, the one real consolation, which is death. From having thought highly of being alive—for, with a few stretches of misery, I have been a fortunate and a happy person,—I began to think highly of being dead. Out of it all. Done with torment. Safe from further piteous woes. My mind, that is, during the drive, ran in directions which the comfortable would call morbid; it ran, in other words, in the direction of stark truth. And I don't see how it could do anything else with a little dead thing, a thing so lately of my intimate acquaintance, which an hour before had been almost fiercely alive and furiously enjoying itself, lying at my feet in the awful meekness of death. Finished, Woosie was; and the manner of his ending left me with a great desire, if only it were possible, to beg his pardon, and the pardon of all poor helpless creatures, for the tragic unkindness of human beings.

I passed a donkey on the way—a small beast, plodding stoutly along, doing his best for the enormous man sitting on a pile of household goods who was driving him. But doing his best didn't save him from being hit. He was hit hard and often. And looking at the man's face, I thought that to an overworked donkey, to a kicked dog, to a pelted cat, it may well seem that this is a world of devils.

Yet there, when I got home, was the familiar heavenly peace of a summer evening in the south. Devils? Such a word was an outrage. The sky was still limpid after a sunset of pure gold. The jagged line of the Esterels, delicate and dark against it, stretched into a sea the colour of pearls. Cypresses, very black and still, stood like solemn witnesses, it might easily be imagined, to the glory of God; and a hush so holy lay over the country-side that it seemed as if the entire world must be at its good-night prayers. It wasn't, of course. Those people in the car, who had killed Woosie, must have got by that time to Monte Carlo, and were probably at anything rather than prayers; and in the peasants' houses, in whose windows lights were beginning to twinkle, there were, from their point of view, few reasons for sending up blessings.

But what *sort* of a world was it, then? I asked myself, looking round at these things in great perplexity and perturbation of spirit. Was its loveliness merely mockery? Was it nothing but a bad joke, played off on its helpless children? Was it just a blanket of beauty drawn across horror, and if a corner were lifted something so terrible would be seen, such suffering and cruelty, that nobody could ever be at peace again?

The gardener helped me bury Woosie. In complete silence we buried him. No questions were asked, and no explanations offered. By the time we had done, the brief southern twilight was over, and the stars were out—

Plainness and clearness without shadow of stain . . .

These poets.

§

Here are my three remaining dogs the following winter —Chunkie in my right arm, Knobbie in my left, Winkie standing, holding on to my knee, and all of them uneasily interested in what the man with the camera was doing:

[200]

They had now become almost painfully precious to
me. Not that I had any fear of their fate being like
Woosie's, for both Knobbie and Winkie were perfectly
obedient, and Chunkie, if he didn't react to orders quite

[*201*]

so instantly, yet was very clever and handy with roads; but after Woosie's death we seemed to draw closer together, in a more undistracted affection. Fights were things of the past. Admonishments grew rusty for want of use. No hand had ever to be lifted. And so greatly did Winkie's intelligence and quickness develop in this atmosphere of peace, that he grew to be really a most remarkable dog.

For instance, what could be more remarkable than his way of dealing, one night, with a highly unpleasant and difficult situation? I was woken up by his getting out of his basket and beginning those heavings which are preliminary to being sick, and at once losing my head, for I had just bought a new carpet, I could think of nothing better to do than to run hither and thither in the room like a distracted hen, first to the door leading on to the balcony, then to the door leading into the passage, unable to decide which would be the best for him to go out of, but very conscious that he must at once go out of something. And he, deeply engaged though he was, yet found time, between two heaves, to turn his head and look at me, exactly as if he were saying, "Don't fuss —this is my affair," and then proceeded, heaving but clear-headed, to my bathroom, where, having placed himself in front of the lavatory, he carefully, skilfully, and deliberately was sick into it.

I hold that it isn't possible not to feel that such a dog is almost painfully precious. And besides his sapience and self-control, he had the added charm of adoring me exclusively. It is a great thing to be adored exclusively. Whenever it has happened in my life, I have liked it very much. And with Winkie it lasted, too; he really did carry out the injunctions of the marriage service, and forsaking all others keep only to me.

Rarely did he take his beautiful, kind eyes off me. When he went to sleep, and was obliged to shut them, he still had the thought of me vivid in his heart, for at my faintest small movement he instantly opened them, and looked at me inquiringly, as if asking whether there was anything I wanted and he could do; and wherever I went there he would be too, and wherever I sat he would jump up and sit beside me—close, protecting me, his head on my knee.

A most dear dog. Of all my dogs, not excluding Coco, he was the one I loved best. And I say was, and I put my love into the past tense, because he is dead.

Fuit. Amavi.

§

Death of Winkie

This story, like life, as it goes on is becoming dotted with graves. It would seem that the more you care for a dog, and the more care you take of him, the more, as it were, he dies. My milkman's dog, who never gets a kind word, and is chained up and half starved, doesn't die; during the whole five years I have been here, an old Alsatian has lain about in the most dangerous places and hasn't been run over; and a hoary *chien de chasse* belonging to the postman, so long past his work that he is hardly able to crawl, still goes on living. Only Winkie dies—Winkie, watched over, guarded, loved and in the heyday of his youth; only he, of all the dogs scattered about everywhere, falls into the clutches of the one tick, among millions of ticks waiting on grass and bushes to fasten on to passing dogs, which is death to catch. And to this story, and to my life, there is added another grave.

Yet, deeply unhappy as his death made me, and for a time quite extraordinarily forlorn, I didn't feel the peculiar distress and horror that swept over me when Woosie died. There was no cruelty, hideous because conscious, behind this death. It isn't possible to be indignant with a tick. Like the rest of us, ticks must live, and nature, having arranged that they shall do so most conveniently to themselves attached to a dog, what is there to be done except try, intelligently and untiringly, to defeat nature? When it comes to ticks, there is no end to my understanding and resignation, nor, after the lesson I have had, is there any end to the skill and patience with which I search for them on my surviving dogs. Unresentfully, but also completely unrelentingly, I track them down, with a zeal so unflagging that it would be a clever tick indeed who should, in future, escape my tweezers.

But this doesn't give me back Winkie, and it is heartbreaking to know that I might have saved him if I had been as skilled, as patient, and as much alive to the danger before he died as I have since become. Through those perilous hot months, April to October, I ought never to have left my dogs; but, supposing all was well with them, for they ate and slept and played as usual, and if Winkie didn't rush about quite as much as the others I merely thought it sensible of him, in such heat— supposing, then, that all was as well as it seemed, I did leave them once during the summer, and went for a jaunt to Corsica.

Why I, who never jaunt, on this occasion did so, was because it was August, and in August I have a birthday, and birthdays, my Pomeranian training taught, are of the utmost importance, and on no account to be ignored. So firm a hold has this teaching got on me that I couldn't ignore it now if I tried. Years pass, yet still, as the day comes round, I feel a stir in me of excitement, of expectation, of an urge to celebrate, of an impulse to do something spectacular; for this, Pomerania insisted and I cannot forget, is the day of days in one's life, a day on which it is a duty, as well as a privilege, to let oneself go.

Accordingly each year I look about me with earnest attentiveness, in search of a direction the letting go can take. But, after a while, there are few directions left which appear sufficiently seemly; and the problem's difficulty is much increased by the fact that I am alone, with no children or husbands to egg me on by setting the day about with candles, and decorating it with cake. I spent my penultimate birthday, so impossible did it seem to find a form of festive activity which should be at the same time reckless and respectable, sulking in bed; and when, on my last one, some young blades of my acquaintance who were at Calvi—female blades, but blades, I take it, can be of either sex,—wrote inviting me to join them in what they described as the most perfect bathing in the world, I jumped at the suggestion as a God-sent solution of my troubles, and without an instant's hesitation let myself go to Corsica.

Corsica is only six hours from Nice by calm sea—by sea which is not calm, considerably more,—Nice is only one hour's drive from me, and off I went, lightheartedly to join other persons of light hearts, and was away a week. A single week, one would think, is not a very long time to leave one's dogs and one's duties, but it had been too long for Winkie, and when I got home he was already past saving.

Still thinking, in my ignorance, that his extreme languor was because of the heat, I asked the vet to give me a tonic for him; but the vet, when he saw him, at once looked at his gums and his tongue, and in a dismay that struck my heart cold said, *"Mais c'est effrayant."*

It was indeed *effrayant*. Winkie's gums and tongue, I now for the first time saw, were almost snow-white, and the vet explained that he had got the fatal tick-disease, the disease more feared than any other in these parts, whose effect is that its victims bleed, internally, to death. Slowly. Each day growing weaker, colder, less able to stand.

§

I will not go into the details of Winkie's dying; it is still too close.

Yesterday, looking out of the window at the darkening garden, where the unaccustomed rain was dripping on yellow leaves, I found my eyes resting on the very place we spent our last few hours together—he lying on a chair, his eyes, grown curiously wise and sad, gazing at the fields he was never to run in again, I sitting on the grass beside him, my hand holding his cold paw, so cold because so bloodless, waiting for the vet, who was coming at six o'clock to put him to sleep; and counting up the weeks, I found there were ten of them since then, and that yesterday was the exact day, ten weeks ago, that he died. So that it is still very close, and cannot well be thought of.

My comfort is that I was able to prevent the suffering of the last stages of this dreadful disease by cutting it short, and I can think of him as never having known real pain. Always, till the very end, when his eyes grew so strangely wise and sad, Winkie had been happy. Nobody ever scolded him. From first to last he heard nothing but words of kindness and of love. His short life was filled with everything a good dog deserves, and its end was quite painless: just a lying down, when I told him to—his final obedience,—with his head on my lap, where he had so often laid it; and then sleep. Before he knew anything different, deep sleep.

§

And now I have got to the end of my fourteenth dog, and with him this record finishes. At the beginning I explained that I have had, altogether, fourteen dogs, and having seen the fourteenth through his brief life, from the day he was born on my bedroom sofa to the day he died on my lap, there is no more to be said.

Here are his bereft parents, watching for him, unable to make out why he doesn't come back.

Every morning, for the first few days after his death, directly they were let out they jumped on to his stool in the garden, from which they could get a better view of the various paths he might come home by. On it they sat patiently together for hours, Knobbie watching one side and Chunkie the other, and hardly to be persuaded to get off it for meals.

And here, a little later, is Chunkie alone with me—

but alone only for three weeks, because Knobbie, most unfortunately just when we most needed the comfort of each other's company, had to go away on her bi-annual visit to the friend who, at such times, keeps her safe from Chunkie's attentions.

On the picture it can be seen that Chunkie is feeling cheerful again. At first, when Knobbie too left him, he was greatly depressed and bewildered, and to console him for his different trials I took him, each afternoon, down to the sea, knowing that he loves bathing and digging holes in the sand; and after a few days of this treatment I observed, with pleasure, that air of Never-say-die, which I have always so much admired in him, reappearing.

Chunkie certainly, whatever I may be, is *resolut*. He, certainly, is ready, after any set-back, to face life again as soon as possible in the proper spirit.

And what is the proper spirit?

Chunkie's, I think—keeping one's end up, and the flag of one's tail briskly flying to the last.

Wise and sensible dog; making the most of what he has, rather than worrying over what he hasn't. And ruminating on the rocks during those afternoons by the sea, it occurred to me that it would be very shameful if I were less sensible, less wholesome, and less sturdy of refusal to go down before blows, than Chunkie.

So I made another vow.

THE END

Other Virago books by Elizabeth von Arnim

THE ENCHANTED APRIL

RECENTLY DRAMATISED ON SCREEN AND FOR
THE BBC

Introduction by Terence de Vere White

A discreet advertisement in *The Times*, addressed to 'those
who Appreciate Wistaria and Sunshine . . .', is the prelude to
a revelatory month for four very different women. High above
a bay on the Italian Riviera stands San Salvatore, a mediæval
castle. Beckoned to this haven are Mrs Wilkins, Mrs
Arbuthnot, Mrs Fisher and Lady Caroline Dester, each
quietly craving a respite. Lulled by the mediterranean spring,
the violet mountains and sweet-scented flowers, they
gradually shed their public skins and discover a harmony
each of them has longed for but none has known. First
published in 1922, reminiscent of *Elizabeth and Her German
Garden*, this delightful novel is imbued with the descriptive
power and light-hearted irreverence for which Elizabeth von
Arnim is so popular.

ELIZABETH AND HER GERMAN GARDEN

Introduction by Elizabeth Jane Howard

'She has a wild sense of comedy and a vision – continually thwarted though it was – of potential happiness' – *Penelope Mortimer*

Indoors are servants, meals and furniture. There, too, is The Man of Wrath, her upright Teutonic husband, inspiring in Elizabeth a mixture of irritation, affection and irreverence. But outside she can escape domestic routine, read favourite books, play with her three babies – and garden to her heart's content. Through Elizabeth's eyes we watch the seasons, from May's 'oasis of bird-cherries and greenery' to the time when 'snow carpets her Pomeranian wilderness'. And each season brings with it new events as friends and neighbours come and go, all wonderfully recorded with Elizabeth's uniquely witty pen.

MR SKEFFINGTON

Approaching the watershed of her fiftieth birthday, Fanny, having long ago divorced Mr Skeffington and dismissed him from her thoughts for many years, is surprised to find herself thinking of him often. While attempting to understand this invasion she meets, through a series of coincidences and deliberate actions, all those other men whose hearts she broke. But their lives have irrevocably changed and Fanny is no longer the exquisite beauty with whom they were all enchanted. If she is to survive, Fanny discovers, she must confront a greatly altered perception of herself.

With the delicate piquancy for which she is renowned, Elizabeth von Arnim here reveals the complexities of emotions involved in the process of ageing and in re-evaluating self-worth.

VERA

Introduction by Xandra Hardie

Lucy Entwhistle's beloved father has just died; aged twenty-two she finds herself alone in the world. Leaning against her garden gate, dazed and unhappy, she is disturbed by the sudden appearance of the perspiring Mr Wemyss. This middle-aged man is also in mourning – for his wife Vera, who has died in mysterious circumstances. Before Lucy can collect herself, Mr Wemyss has taken charge: of the funeral arrangements, of her kind aunt Dot, but most of all of Lucy herself – body and soul. Elizabeth von Arnim's masterpiece, *Vera* (1921), is a forceful study of the power of men in marriage, and the weakness of women when they love.

THE CARAVANERS

Introduction by Kate Saunders

For the Major and his wife Edelgard, the idea of a
caravanning holiday in Southern England seems perfect. As
they begin their leisurely progress through its green and
verdant countryside, the holiday spirit sets in. But England
presents more than just a contrast of scenery to this German
couple – amongst the company of their English companions
Edelgard seems to undergo a change of temperament,
revealing herself to be far less biddable than the upright
Major had believed. The blossoming of the hedgerows is one
thing, but the blossoming of his wife is quite another . . .

THE ADVENTURES OF ELIZABETH IN RÜGEN

Introduction by Penelope Mortimer

When a drought threatens Elizabeth's beloved garden, she is tempted to explore the island of Rügen, off Germany's Baltic coast, with its innumerable amber bays and chalk cliffs crowned by splendid beechwoods. But Elizabeth soon finds her tour, with maid, coachman and carriage, complicated by unforeseen hazards, including a snobbish bishop's wife with her handsome son, long-lost cousin Charlotte, and her deserted husband, the maddeningly genial old Professor.

CHRISTOPHER AND COLUMBUS

As the First World War looms, Anna-Rose and
Anna-Felicitas, seventeen-year-old orphan twins, are thrust
upon relatives. But Uncle Arthur, a blustering patriot, is a
reluctant guardian: the twins are half-German and, who
knows, they could be spying from the nursery window . . .
Packed off to America, they meet Mr Twist, a wealthy
engineer with a tendency to motherliness, who befriends
them on the voyage. However, he has failed to consider the
pitfalls of taking such young and beautiful women under his
wing, especially two who will continue to require his
protection long after the ship has docked, and who are
incapable of behaving with tact. Many adventures ensue (and
befall them) in this sparklingly witty, romantic novel in which
Elizabeth von Arnim explores the suspicions cast upon the
two Annas and Mr Twist in a country poised for war.

LOVE

Introduction by Terence de Vere White

Catherine becomes aware of Christopher on her fifth visit to
The Immortal Hour, playing to empty houses at King's Cross.
It is his thirty-second. He is a glorious young man with
flame-coloured hair. She is the sweetest little thing in a hat.
Some performances later, they are sitting side by side and all
seems set for the perfect romance – but for the small matter of
age. Chris is in the first flush of manhood and Catherine is
just a *little* bit older. For a woman in her forties, with
marriage and motherhood behind her, the notion of being
thought younger than her years adds an extra thrill to
courtship. But there are unforeseen obstacles to such
pleasures . . . Beneath the humour of this engaging novel,
originally published in 1925, lies a sharper note, as Elizabeth
von Arnim uncovers the hypocrisy of society and the codes it
forces women to ascribe to in the name of 'love'.

THE PASTOR'S WIFE

Ingeborg Bullivant, the put-upon daughter of the Bishop of Redchester, suddenly becomes possessed by the demon Rebellion and takes a week's tour to Lucerne. Constantly in the company of a ponderous German pastor, she is put into a quandary when he proposes marriage. Faced with her father's wrath on her return, however, Ingeborg accepts Herr Dremmel with simple relief. But the role of a pastor's wife in East Prussia is not as Ingeborg had imagined – for she has merely exchanged one set of rules for another. Ingeborg's experiences are recounted here with subtlety and humour, yet beneath Elizabeth von Arnim's characteristic wit is her recurrent theme: the bondage of women as daughters and wives, never more deftly explored than in this accomplished novel, first published in 1914.